Digital Innovations in Architecture, Engineering and Construction

The Architecture, Engineering and Construction (AEC) industry is experiencing an unprecedented transformation from conventional labor-intensive activities to automation using innovative digital technologies and processes. This new paradigm also requires systemic changes focused on social, economic and sustainability aspects. Within the scope of Industry 4.0, digital technologies are a key factor in interconnecting information between the physical built environment and the digital virtual ecosystem. The most advanced virtual ecosystems allow to simulate the built to enable a real-time data-driven decision-making. This Book Series promotes and expedites the dissemination of recent research, advances, and applications in the field of digital innovations in the AEC industry. Topics of interest include but are not limited to:

- Industrialization: digital fabrication, modularization, cobotics, lean.
- Material innovations: bio-inspired, nano and recycled materials.
- Reality capture: computer vision, photogrammetry, laser scanning, drones.
- Extended reality: augmented, virtual and mixed reality.
- Sustainability and circular building economy.
- Interoperability: building/city information modeling.
- Interactive and adaptive architecture.
- Computational design: data-driven, generative and performance-based design.
- Simulation and analysis: digital twins, virtual cities.
- Data analytics: artificial intelligence, machine/deep learning.
- Health and safety: mobile and wearable devices, QR codes, RFID.
- Big data: GIS, IoT, sensors, cloud computing.
- Smart transactions, cybersecurity, gamification, blockchain.
- Quality and project management, business models, legal prospective.
- Risk and disaster management.

Arianna Latini

Immersive Virtual Reality for a Building Occupant-Centric Design

Defining, Validating and Applying an Innovative Framework

Springer

Arianna Latini
DICEA
Università Politecnica delle Marche
Ancona, Italy

ISSN 2731-7269 ISSN 2731-7277 (electronic)
Digital Innovations in Architecture, Engineering and Construction
ISBN 978-3-031-66027-6 ISBN 978-3-031-66028-3 (eBook)
https://doi.org/10.1007/978-3-031-66028-3

This Springer imprint is published by the registered company Springer Nature Switzerland AG
The registered company address is: Gewerbestrasse 11, 6330 Cham, Switzerland

Preface

Currently, people spend most of their time in enclosed spaces. Hence, a crucial aspect is to create sustainable and conducive indoor environments for the health and well-being of the people. Even if the human dimension is at the forefront of concern in building design and regulation, the comprehension of human responses to indoor environmental factors is oversimplified. The reason is that individuals are exposed to several indoor variables at a time and there is a scarcity of multi-domain analysis looking for the effect of all these variables at a time. A significant barrier to the acceleration of knowledge in this field is the difficulty of controlling and testing different and multiple stimuli in laboratory-based studies in terms of the amount of time and resources needed for the setup which limits the generalizability of the outcomes to real-life contexts.

To this end, Virtual Reality and Immersive Virtual Environments are suggested as alternative methods to facilitate the exploration of this research domain and leverage the adoption of advanced methodologies and experimental approaches to address and improve the human dimension in buildings.

This book discusses the cutting-edge intersection of Virtual Reality and Building Occupants Research. It presents an innovative way of using Virtual Environments and Virtual Reality to revolutionise the comprehension of human-dimension responses to indoor built environment variations. A robust, innovative and sequential protocol is defined and validated with a Virtual Environment against a real-world counterpart to provide readers with methodological approaches suitable for carrying out rigorous experimental research in Building Occupant Research. This comprehensive guide provides also practical applications of the proposed guidelines to show the potential and effectiveness of Virtual Reality for conducting studies in different indoor environmental conditions in a multi-sensory approach. This book serves as a resource for researchers who want to exploit the full potential of Virtual Reality in collecting reliable data useful for understanding human dimensions within built environments.

The present work arises from 4 years of doctorate experience in coupling human-building interaction, comfort, work efficiency and behaviour research with technological innovation finding the *trait d'union* in the Immersive Virtual Reality framework.

The author would like to thank Prof. Marco D'Orazio and Prof. Elisa Di Giuseppe for the extraordinary guidance, freedom and trust they placed in this research and during the development of the book. Special thanks to Dr. Samantha Di Loreto and Prof. Costanzo Di Perna for their support in the experimental activity concerning "Varying the Acoustical Environment" presented in Chap. 5. A heartfelt gratitude to Dr. Ludovica Marcelli, Dr. Simone Torresin, Dr. Tin Oberman, Prof. Francesco Aletta and Prof. Jian Kang for the collaboration in the experimental activity concerning "Combining Visual and Acoustical variation" related to the Biophilic Design strategies discussed in Chap. 6.

Ancona, Italy Arianna Latini

Contents

Chapter 1
Introduction

Abstract Research on Building Occupants is challenging due to the complexities of multi-domain analysis and the limitations of traditional laboratory settings. Virtual Reality and Immersive Virtual Environments offer advanced solutions for studying the human dimension in buildings. Despite the proven potential of these solutions, the lack of standardized protocols and reliable data collection methods limits their broader use. As a result, this book proposes a novel experimental framework to integrate Virtual Reality technology into Building Occupant Research and support researchers in effectively adopting these solutions to conduct multi-domain studies. The framework is validated through immersive models and empirical studies, demonstrating the effectiveness of Virtual Reality and Immersive Virtual Environments in producing reliable data and supporting evidence-based design practices.

The building and construction supply chain represents one of the world's largest industry sectors. *Buildings* are designed by people and for people to live and work in, and building occupants constantly affect and are affected by buildings, in a bidirectional relationship. As an example, the precondition for human activity is the *building design* which might either support or limit individual tasks while shaping occupants' perceptions, experiences, and behaviour. Smart buildings have the potential to facilitate the shift toward a more sustainable paradigm coupled with technological innovation to decrease energy use and improve indoor quality. However, technological progress and investments alone rarely guarantee low or net-zero energy in buildings because «human factors» play a crucial role.

Nowadays, people are spending more than 20 h per day inside buildings, where almost all human activities take place from professional to personal ones. Over the last decades, there has been a growing interest in the influence of indoor environmental conditions on *individuals*. As a result, the creation of positive impacts on people is fundamental for professionals, researchers and policymakers by providing long-term value and quality of life to reduce operating use and energy-related costs while optimizing well-being and work efficiency.

An imperative concern for building standards and certifications has emerged shifting an overall interest and scientific attention to the suitability of the building

A. Latini, *Immersive Virtual Reality for a Building Occupant-Centric Design*, Digital Innovations in Architecture, Engineering and Construction,
https://doi.org/10.1007/978-3-031-66028-3_1

sector for health and well-being issues. There is a global imperative for a *user-centred design approach* in the Architectural, Engineering, and Construction sectors. However, understanding and empowering the so-called *human-building interaction* is often oversimplified in the building life cycle, due to the stochastic, complex, and interdisciplinary nature of occupants' comfort and behaviour.

A growing body of research is demonstrating the relevant impact of environmental conditions on individuals' perception, comfort, work efficiency and behaviour which are multimodal and influenced by the combination of stimuli associated with different domains, namely thermal, acoustic, visual, and air quality. To establish an acceptable indoor environment, the effects of all the sensory variables and environmental factors that can realistically be found within buildings should be considered in *multisensory integration*. Bridging this gap through scientific research can lead to enhanced design practices and guidelines.

However, there is a scarcity of multi-domain analysis looking for the effect of all these variables at a time. A significant barrier to the acceleration of knowledge in this field is the difficulty of controlling and testing different stimuli in laboratory-based studies in terms of the amount of time and resources needed for the setup which limits the generalizability of the results to real-life contexts.

To this end, *Virtual Reality* (VR) and *Immersive Virtual Environments* (IVE) are suggested as alternative methods to facilitate the exploration of this research domain and leverage the adoption of advanced methodologies and experimental approaches to address and improve the human dimension in buildings.

To date, there is a lack of a protocol and standardized methods to carry out experiments in VR and collect reliable data. These issues prevent the diffusion of VR for the comprehension of human-dimension and support evidence-based design.

As a result, this book proposed a novel experimental framework to organise, carry out and enhance the adoption of VR technology in *Building Occupant Research*. The aim is to support researchers in how to strategically and effectively adopt VR technology and to demonstrate the effectiveness of such a methodological approach and its potential to support multi-domain studies.

Chapter 2 gives a comprehensive overview of the background and context in which the book takes shape, concerning the human dimension in *Building Occupant Research*. Chapter 3 provides the state of knowledge about Immersive Virtual Reality applications in the scientific fields of building occupants focusing on its suitability as a research tool and describing the most frequently used data collection methods for investigating the human dimension. It pictures the research gap in the adoption of Virtual Reality to support human dimension research in buildings.

To address these challenges a step-by-step experimental framework is defined in Chap. 4, design research guidelines and the suitability of the protocol and Virtual Reality as research tools are validated by generating an immersive virtual model and comparing it with its real counterpart (Chap. 5). In Chap. 6, the author addresses the successful application of the developed experimental method in empirical studies. Specifically, the purpose is to provide evidence about the potential of using this method for the investigation of human dimension in indoor built environments producing trustworthy data suitable to allow the researcher to make general conclusions and further support building design practises and theories.

Chapter 2
Building Occupant Research

Abstract The built environment is a pivotal determinant of occupants' health and well-being, influencing their overall quality of life. The COVID-19 pandemic has leveraged the interest toward a more conducive, comfortable and healthy indoor space for individuals promoting transformative changes in design guidelines. With people spending a huge amount of daily time indoors, the need for a supportive indoor environment has never been more urgent, particularly considering the resulting economic implications of indoor environmental quality. Integrating human factors into building decision-making phases and design is essential for delivering more user-centred and efficient buildings. In Building Occupant Research, empirical assessments, including in-situ monitoring campaigns and laboratory-based studies, are crucial to gather evidence-based design guidelines. Despite recent technological advancements, gaps persist in a scarcity of multi-domain assessments to consider multiple and multisensorial indoor environmental characteristics simultaneously. Indeed, challenges related to the complexity of data collection methods in physical settings and the limited generalizability of results emerged. A possible solution could be the implementation of more technological innovations into empirical assessment methods, developing suitable knowledge to support evidence-based design guidelines and a user-centred approach.

2.1 The Building Sector and the Occupant-Centric Design

The building and construction supply chain represents one of the world's largest industry sectors [1].

Buildings are designed by people and for people to live and work in, and building occupants constantly affect and are affected by buildings, in a bidirectional relationship. Indeed, evidence suggests that on one side occupant behaviour has significant impacts on building use and energy consumption and on the other changes in the built environment impact the human state of mind and corresponding reactions [2].

A. Latini, *Immersive Virtual Reality for a Building Occupant-Centric Design*, Digital Innovations in Architecture, Engineering and Construction,
https://doi.org/10.1007/978-3-031-66028-3_2

As an example, the precondition for human activity is the building design which might, for example, either support or limit individual tasks while shaping occupants' perceptions, experiences, and behaviour.

Considering the relevant contribution of the building sector and the current environmental concerns, buildings have the potential to facilitate the shift toward a more sustainable paradigm coupled with technological innovation. The new generation of smart buildings has the potential to decrease energy use and improve indoor quality levels. However, technological progress and investments alone rarely guarantee low or net-zero energy in buildings because *human factors* play a crucial role.

As a result, the creation of positive impacts on people by providing long-term value and quality of life is fundamental to reducing operating use and energy-related costs while optimizing well-being and work efficiency.

Currently, professionals, researchers and policymakers believe that the most effective way to enhance building performance and achieve energy efficiency at a large scale is through the advancement of building codes and standards and increased attention to the human dimension.

Thus, a shift forward in the inclusion of the human dimension in building performance assessments and practice emerged. Evident is the rise of concern of building rating (e.g., ASHRAE Standard 55, EN 16,798-1:2019, UNI EN ISO 7730:2006), and certifications (e.g., LEED, WorldGBC), which originally focused on Indoor Environmental Quality (air quality, thermal comfort, lighting, acoustics), interior layout and ergonomics, while are now increasingly shifting to health and wellbeing issues (e.g., WELL Standard), thus catalysing a global interest and scientific attention to the suitability of the building sector.

A worldwide imperative for the Architectural, Engineering and Construction sectors is the application of a *Building Occupant-Centric or Human-Centric Design approach*. By giving end-users extensive attention at each stage of the design process and building life cycle, it will be possible to create comfortable and supportive indoor environments that inspire, energize, and support people using it.

However, understanding and empowering the so-called *human-building interaction* is often oversimplified in the building life cycle, due to the stochastic, complex, and interdisciplinary nature of occupants' comfort and behaviour.

2.2 The Significance of the Built Environment on Occupants

There can hardly be anything more important than our health and wellbeing and the built environment has a major influence on our quality of daily life.

The impact of the COVID-19 pandemic has enhanced the interest in the influence of the built environment on occupants and had a transformative impact on the design and operation of buildings for a more sustainable and conducive building.

In this context, the high attention building occupants research topic is driven by several factors. Firstly, there is a growing awareness of the importance of creating comfortable, supportive, and healthy indoor environments. The main reason is that, nowadays, people are spending more than 20 h per day inside buildings [3], which is why, over the last decades, there has been an increasing interest in the impact of indoor environmental conditions on individuals. Secondly, this is a very relevant topic as the role that indoor environments can play on users' health, well-being, comfort, behaviour, and work efficiency has never been more evident. It was estimated by the World Health Organization, that 19% of the factors influencing individuals' health and well-being are directly related to the characteristics of the built environment [4].

In addition, adults spend a significant amount of their time in working environments (60–70% every week) [4] where they constantly try to provide comfortable and supportive working conditions. The workplace environment can be beneficial or detrimental to occupants' satisfaction, performance, and well-being [4, 5]. As a result, there is an upward recognition of the economic implications and benefits of indoor environmental quality. In recent years, the increasing awareness of benefits deriving from enhanced work efficiency shifted higher emphasis on providing valuable indoor environmental quality within office buildings. In particular, workspace design affects not only people's well-being but also their work performance linked to business-oriented outputs and is especially relevant in personnel costs [6]. Workers' salaries and benefits typically account for 90% of a company's costs [7, 8]. The comfort factors of office users regard physical comfort and functional comfort [8]. They refer to biological responses (e.g., light, indoor air quality, climate, noise, ergonomics) and the suitability of work environments for work tasks (e.g., disturbances and distractions). Even a slight improvement in comfort can have a fundamental impact on individual task-related performance.

A challenge in how to objectively and rigorously insight and quantify the features that improve comfort, behaviour and work efficiency in indoor spaces arises. In this context, actions based on comprehensive multi-sensory evidence are required to extensively improve the human dimension outcomes while maximising building efficiency.

Considering the potential impact of individuals on buildings and vice versa, empowered data, theories, guidelines, and models are essential to leverage human dimensions in significantly reducing building energy use and improving indoor quality of life during the entire building life cycle. More than ever, the imperative challenge is improving the understanding of human needs, comfort, work efficiency and behaviour while encouraging the reduction of operating costs and energy and developing suitable strategies to aid economic and environmental targets.

2.3 Traditional Methods and Gaps

Empirical assessments are the basis of evidence-based practices, theories on the human dimension and mathematical equations for building performance simulation programs. A fundamental role is played by *in-field monitoring campaigns and laboratory experiments* with controlled environmental conditions [9]. By conducting experiments in these research facilities, scientists can gather data about individuals and buildings. Different sources of data storage include, for example, built environmental measures (e.g., CO_2, air temperature, humidity, light, air velocity sensors), wearable sensors for physiological measures (e.g., electro-dermal activity, skin temperature, heart rate) [10, 11] and surveys to evaluate subjective sensations of occupants [12]. Experimental processes are carried out every day by researchers, but only comprehensive assessments could bring valuable results in the field of Human-Centric comfort, work efficiency and behaviour studies in the long term.

Over the past years in Building Occupant Research, many efforts have been devoted to studying the human dimension mainly acknowledging the impact of standalone indoor environmental stimuli on individuals. However, building occupants perception, health, well-being, behaviour and performance are influenced by the simultaneous presence of multiple indoor environmental stimuli, such as thermal, lighting, acoustic, air quality and layout. To establish an acceptable indoor environment, the effects of all the sensory variables and environmental factors that can realistically be found within buildings should be considered in a multisensory integration [13]. In response to that, «multi-domain approaches» to support an effective understanding of indoor environmental impacts in behavioural research [14] have been proposed as one of the main areas of interest of IEA EBC Annex 79 [15]. Multi-domain studies include two types of effect investigated [13]: *cross-modal effect* when one stimulus influences a non-related response triggered by another stimulus (e.g. when temperature influences visual or acoustical responses); *combined effect* when multiple combined stimuli affect a response not directly related to a specific indoor stimulus (i.e., perception, behaviour, physiology, and performance in presence of visual stimuli combined with acoustical scenarios). Conversely, the *same-modality effect* is typical of single-domain studies, referring to the influence of one domain (e.g., lighting conditions) on the same-modality response (e.g., visual comfort).

However, current building regulations and guidelines are based on knowledge built upon single-domain studies [13]. Therefore, crucial gaps in scientific knowledge exist due to the need to boost human comfort research through multi-domain analysis. ASHRAE Guideline 10P [16] emphasized the interactions among indoor environmental factors and recommended that more detailed research might be conducted. Indeed, the observed discrepancies between predicted and reported occupant satisfaction, comfort and work efficiency could be explained by a lack of multisensory integration [13].

Furthermore, the possibility of accounting for the centrality of multi-domain approaches in indoor building context and scientific research opens the way to new

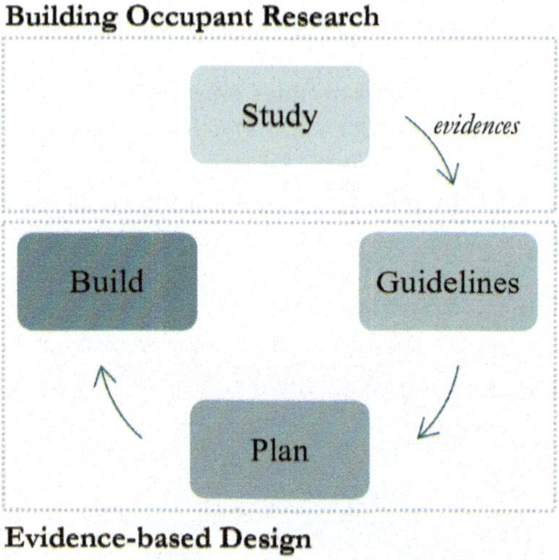

Fig. 2.1 The foundation of building design is the evidence provided by scientific research

opportunities: a deeper understanding of human responses (i.e., comfort, work efficiency, behaviour) to their complex surrounding environment and a more tangible possibility of ensuring sustainable and conducive buildings to the health and well-being of the people. Collected and interpreted measures will be the optimised evidence basis to marry enhanced design practices and guidelines on this topic [14]. These "proofs" from scientific research will be translated into design guidelines and building standards to encourage not arbitrary design choices in a variety-built environment practice (Fig. 2.1).

Additionally, sufficient insight and adequate representation of the complex human dimension in building simulation tools could contribute to filling the gaps between the designed and actual energy performance [17]. Including human knowledge in building systems and maintenance is also the key aspect of delivering user-centred and personalised building systems capable of supporting the optimal operation of buildings, reducing energy consumption and increasing efficiency [18].

In this context, two main factors underpin the challenge observed in Building Occupants Research. Firstly, multi-domain assessment of indoor environmental characteristics remains in large parts understudied with heterogeneous methodological approaches and inconsistent results to support evidence-based design guidelines, building performance models and theories. Secondly, manipulations of indoor environment variables are often costly and logistically challenging to implement in real monitoring campaigns or laboratory experiments which lead to human responses that may not be fully generalizable to real-life contexts.

Data collection is the most time-consuming and costly phase of a research project, and, due to the complexity and variety of variables included in the human-building context, researchers may find it difficult to conduct a comprehensive analysis. Indeed, it is common to conduct investigations for each stimulus, considering, for instance, visual, thermal, acoustic, and air quality separately (an example is provided in Fig. 2.2).

Thus, several troubles emerged: findings remain tenuous due to the unique site-specific nature of each study, the impossibility of replicating a wide range of contexts, carrying out analysis for buildings still under design, and customising experimental models by modifying the multiple variables in a short time [19, 20].

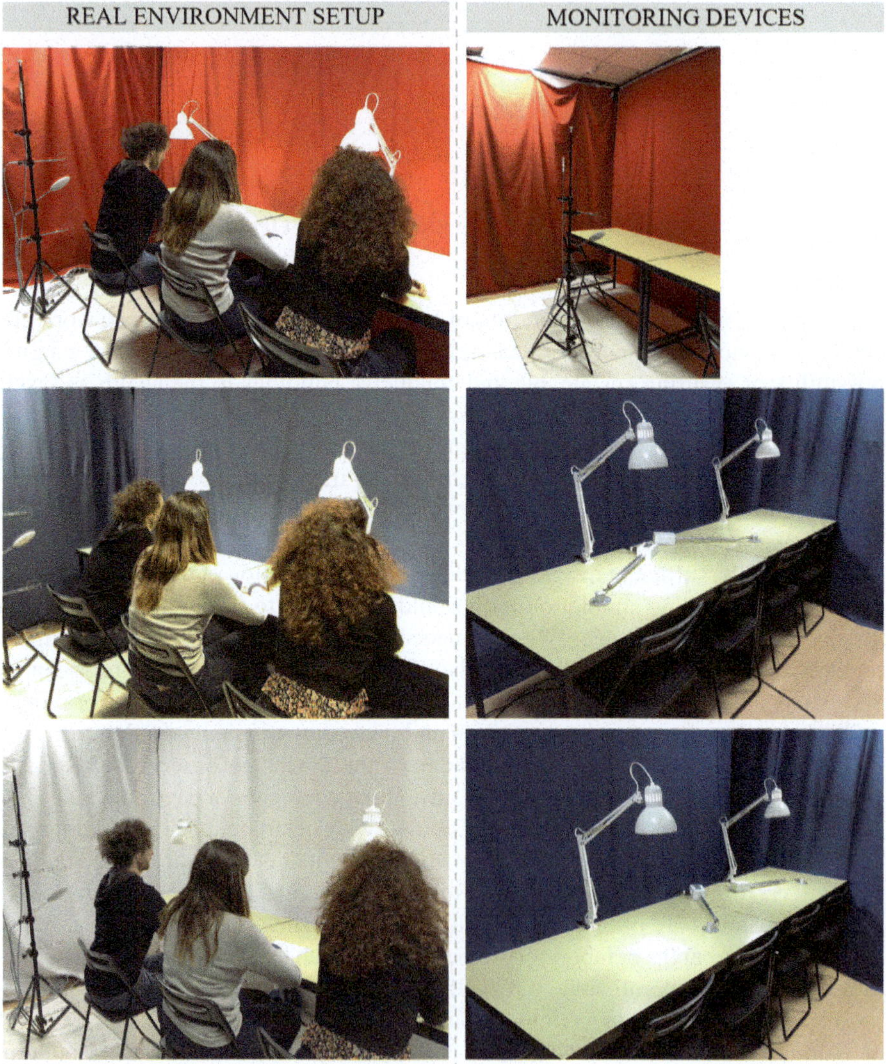

Fig. 2.2 Examples of traditional experimental activity for studying indoor layout variations concerning walls colour. Photographs of the author

These criticalities limit the generalizability of the results to real-life contexts. Consequently, evaluations of human responses could not be free from ecological validity issues and produce evidence that is increasingly complex and sometimes contradictory.

A possible solution could be the incorporation of more technological innovations into empirical assessment methods to gather a significantly higher amount of data producing a better knowledge suitable to define design guidelines and user-centred building systems.

References

1. F. Barbosa, J. Woetzel, J. Mischke, M.J.J. Ribeirinho, M. Sridhar, M. Parsons, N. Bertram, S. Brown, MCKINSEY GLOBAL INSTITUTE, Reinventing Construction: A Route To Higher Productivity, McKinsey Glob. Inst. (2017) 168.
2. International Energy Agency, Annex 66 Final Report: Proposal Definition and Simulation of Occupant Behavior in Buildings Definition and Simulation of Occupant Behavior in Buildings, 2014.
3. European Ventilation Industry Association, Evia's Eu Manifesto: Good Indoor Air Quality Is a Basic Human Right, 2019.
4. H. Coolican, Research Methods and Statistics in Psychology, 2018. https://doi.org/10.4324/9781315201009.
5. Y. Al Horr, M. Arif, A. Kaushik, A. Mazroei, M. Katafygiotou, E. Elsarrag, Occupant productivity and office indoor environment quality: A review of the literature, Build. Environ. 105 (2016) 369–389. https://doi.org/10.1016/j.buildenv.2016.06.001.
6. ASHRAE Standard, Journal - June 2019, 61 (2019) 1–85.
7. World Green building Council, Health, wellbeing & Productivity in Offices, World Green Build. Counc. 1 (2014) 46.
8. A. Feige, H. Wallbaum, M. Janser, L. Windlinger, Impact of sustainable office buildings on occupant's comfort and productivity, J. Corp. Real Estate. 15 (2013) 7–34. https://doi.org/10.1108/JCRE-01-2013-0004.
9. F. Vittori, C. Chiatti, I. Pigliautile, A.L. Pisello, The NEXT.ROOM: Design principles and systems trials of a novel test room aimed at deepening our knowledge on human comfort, Build. Environ. 211 (2022) 108744. https://doi.org/10.1016/j.buildenv.2021.108744.
10. I. Pigliautile, S. Casaccia, N. Morresi, M. Arnesano, A.L. Pisello, G.M. Revel, Assessing occupants' personal attributes in relation to human perception of environmental comfort: Measurement procedure and data analysis, Build. Environ. 177 (2020) 106901. https://doi.org/10.1016/j.buildenv.2020.106901.
11. B. Dong, V. Prakash, F. Feng, Z. O'Neill, A review of smart building sensing system for better indoor environment control, Energy Build. 199 (2019) 29–46. https://doi.org/10.1016/j.enbuild.2019.06.025.
12. B.F. Balvedi, E. Ghisi, R. Lamberts, A review of occupant behaviour in residential buildings, Energy Build. 174 (2018) 495–505. https://doi.org/10.1016/j.enbuild.2018.06.049.
13. G. Chinazzo, R.K. Andersen, E. Azar, V.M. Barthelmes, C. Becchio, L. Belussi, C. Berger, S. Carlucci, S.P. Corgnati, S. Crosby, L. Danza, L. de Castro, M. Favero, S. Gauthier, R.T. Hellwig, Q. Jin, J. Kim, M. Sarey Khanie, D. Khovalyg, C. Lingua, A. Luna-Navarro, A. Mahdavi, C. Miller, I. Mino-Rodriguez, I. Pigliautile, A.L. Pisello, R.F. Rupp, A.-M. Sadick, F. Salamone, M. Schweiker, M. Syndicus, G. Spigliantini, N.G. Vasquez, D. Vakalis, M. Vellei, S. Wei, Quality criteria for multi-domain studies in the indoor environment: Critical review towards research guidelines and recommendations, Build. Environ. 226 (2022) 109719. https://doi.org/10.1016/j.buildenv.2022.109719.

14. M. Schweiker, E. Ampatzi, M.S. Andargie, R.K. Andersen, E. Azar, V.M. Barthelmes, C. Berger, L. Bourikas, S. Carlucci, G. Chinazzo, L.P. Edappilly, M. Favero, S. Gauthier, A. Jamrozik, M. Kane, A. Mahdavi, C. Piselli, A.L. Pisello, A. Roetzel, A. Rysanek, K. Sharma, S. Zhang, Review of multi-domain approaches to indoor environmental perception and behaviour, Build. Environ. 176 (2020) 106804. https://doi.org/10.1016/j.buildenv.2020.106804.
15. W. O'Brien, A. Wagner, M. Schweiker, A. Mahdavi, J. Day, M.B. Kjærgaard, S. Carlucci, B. Dong, F. Tahmasebi, D. Yan, T. Hong, H.B. Gunay, Z. Nagy, C. Miller, C. Berger, Introducing IEA EBC annex 79: Key challenges and opportunities in the field of occupant-centric building design and operation, Build. Environ. 178 (2020) 106738. https://doi.org/10.1016/j.buildenv.2020.106738.
16. R. and A.-C.E. American Society of Heating, ANSI/ASHRAE Guideline 10: Interactions affecting the achievement of acceptable indoor environments., (2011).
17. S. D'Oca, T. Hong, J. Langevin, The human dimensions of energy use in buildings: A review, Renew. Sustain. Energy Rev. 81 (2018) 731–742. https://doi.org/10.1016/j.rser.2017.08.019.
18. M.V. Bavaresco, S. D'Oca, E. Ghisi, R. Lamberts, Technological innovations to assess and include the human dimension in the building-performance loop: A review, Energy Build. 202 (2019). https://doi.org/10.1016/j.enbuild.2019.109365.
19. C. Chokwitthaya, Y. Zhu, S. Mukhopadhyay, E. Collier, Augmenting building performance predictions during design using generative adversarial networks and immersive virtual environments, Autom. Constr. 119 (2020) 103350. https://doi.org/10.1016/j.autcon.2020.103350.
20. S. Kalantari, J.R.J. Neo, Virtual Environments for Design Research: Lessons Learned From Use of Fully Immersive Virtual Reality in Interior Design Research, J. Inter. Des. 45 (2020) 27–42. https://doi.org/10.1111/joid.12171.

Chapter 3
Immersive Virtual Reality in Buildings Occupant Research

Abstract Virtual Reality and Immersive Virtual Environments are suggested as alternative and innovative methods to traditional experimental settings in Building Occupants Research. These low-cost technologies thanks to the speed execution allow replication of tests and users to be immersed in a 1:1 scaled environment, while researchers collect real-time feedback and easily control the design variables. They offer a versatile and powerful tool for evaluating indoor environments and measuring human factors. Typical dependent variables collected during these experiments include subjective assessment of individuals' perception, comfort, and emotional state, while objective measures include physiological and cognitive responses. Despite the advantages offered by Virtual Reality and the growing amount of research conducted in this area, there remains a limited understanding of how multiple indoor environmental conditions influence occupants. This is due to several challenges which currently harm its adoption to support evidence-based design practices and improve indoor environments for individuals, including the need for validation studies, limited attention to multi-domain research, inconsistent methodologies and study design.

3.1 Definition and Concept

Although a substantial amount of research has produced metrics regarding human comfort, work efficiency and behavioural patterns, determining which attributes of the indoor environment matter most to building occupants, there is a limited and inadequate understanding of how multiple indoor environmental conditions influence occupants.

A significant barrier to the acceleration of knowledge in this field is the *difficulty of controlling the variation of indoor environmental conditions in multi-domain studies based on real environment experiments.* This is an acknowledged issue.

To this end, Virtual Reality (VR), Virtual Environments (VEs) and Immersive Virtual Environments or Immersive Virtual Reality (IVEs, IVR) are suggested as alternative methods that can facilitate the exploration of this research domain and

A. Latini, *Immersive Virtual Reality for a Building Occupant-Centric Design*, Digital Innovations in Architecture, Engineering and Construction,
https://doi.org/10.1007/978-3-031-66028-3_3

leverage the adoption of innovative and advanced methodologies, tools and experimental approaches to address and improve users' well-being, behaviour and working efficiency in buildings.

The Oxford English Dictionary first used the term "virtual reality" in the 1980s but, at first, the devices were not efficient, cumbersome, and expensive. At the end of the century, as underlying technologies have become more established, the use of the term has shifted. Indeed, the US National Research Council stated [1]: "Virtual Reality refers to a set of techniques for creating synthetic, computer-generated environments in which human operators can become immersed. In Virtual Reality systems, human operators are connected to computers that can simulate a wide variety of worlds, both real and imaginary, and can interact with those worlds through a variety of sensory channels and manipulators. [..] More sophisticated systems, such as those used for pilot training and immersive entertainment experiences, can include head-mounted displays".

Virtual Environments are simulated environments created to provide users with a sensory experience similar to that of being in a real or unreal place. They can have different levels of complexity and may include elements such as visual, auditory, olfactory and tactile. Virtual Environments can be experienced through various VR systems: non-immersive (e.g., screen-based interaction with 3D graphics), partially immersive (e.g., visors, CAVE), and fully immersive [2]. As a result, *Immersive Virtual Environments* (IVE) or *Immersive Virtual Reality* (IVR) are Virtual Environments that fully immerse users in a simulated world who will perceive themselves as enclosed in the virtual world, allowing a strong sense of presence and involvement.

Four are the main concepts and characteristics related to VR and hence essential towards validation of its conclusions, as hereunder discussed:

- *Immersion* indicates the "state in which a participant becomes attracted and involved in a virtual space of an activity to an extension that his or her mind is separated from the physical space he or she is being active in" [3]. The level of immersion strictly depends on visual realism, display parameters, haptics, and sound [2]. It is also linked to the degree of the user's interaction with the virtual environment and to the realism of the study [4].
- *Presence* is concomitant with immersion since it refers to "the sense of being in an environment" [3]. The idea of presence in Virtual Environments is the sense of being in places where the Virtual Reality suggests, rather than the physical location. Sense of presence within a Virtual Environment is mainly investigated with self-reporting questionnaires.
- *Users' experience* could be influenced by the narrative used during or before the experiments (i.e., introductory demo sessions, short adaptation phases) and by cybersickness which describes symptoms (e.g., headache, nausea, or dizziness) experienced by users during VR sessions [5].
- *Ecological Validity* indicates the ability to make general conclusions from experimental results equivalent to those conducted in real-life situations as well as the realistic behavioural response of participants. It is a crucial point, namely for researchers that use VE as a predictive tool [3]. Comparing the results of an

experiment conducted in both a real and virtual environment is a common method for testing ecological validity. The absence of statistical difference between the outcomes validates the VE and allows researchers to generalize the findings [4].

Recent significant strides in hardware and software, allowed Virtual Reality to decrease in size, become cost-effective and provide the users a greater immersion in terms of sight, hearing and the possibility to interact with virtual objects. Thanks to the technological advances in audio, graphics and rendering, Immersive Virtual Environments have been developed and widely used from simple means of entertainment into effective and reliable allies in research. Due to these significant strides, Virtual Reality embraces several fields (e.g., medical disorders treatment, industrial applications, training experience) attracting the attention of professionals and academia and permitting the tool to transcend the technology field.

3.2 Advantages

The built environment, the human dimension and Virtual Reality technology have been the focus of recent Building Occupants Research. The Architectural, Engineering, and Construction sectors have acknowledged VR for its capacity to create multisensory 3D environments that immerse the user in a virtual world [6].

VR can help to visualise the design of a site/building before its construction, resulting in cost savings and better outcomes, above all in case Building Information Modelling submissions are converted into VR. The potentialities lie in supporting experts to identify the pros and cons of design decisions while having a better understanding of the outcomes; enabling the revision of the planning and the monitoring of the progress more efficiently [7]; facilitating the communication of design details and scopes via the creation of immersive virtual models that allow stakeholders to experience an unbuilt or under maintenance indoor or outdoor environment from a first-person point of view [8]. Well-developed Immersive Virtual Environments could ensure a sense of presence with high ecological validity, playing a leading role in the evaluation and prediction of real-world human responses [9].

The use of these technologies is not only limited to the design phase but can also provide several advantages over other traditional data collection methods in this research domain, such as traditional empirical assessment. Much more complex, immersive, and extensive design possibilities are offered by IVEs. Indeed, by involving study participants in complex physical and social environments that are ecologically valid, researchers can improve their comprehension of environmental designs.

The human-building research core process can be positively and drastically changed by VR and IVEs. Researchers and designers are observing an increase in support and improvement concerning the acquisition and integration of human factors from the early design stage.

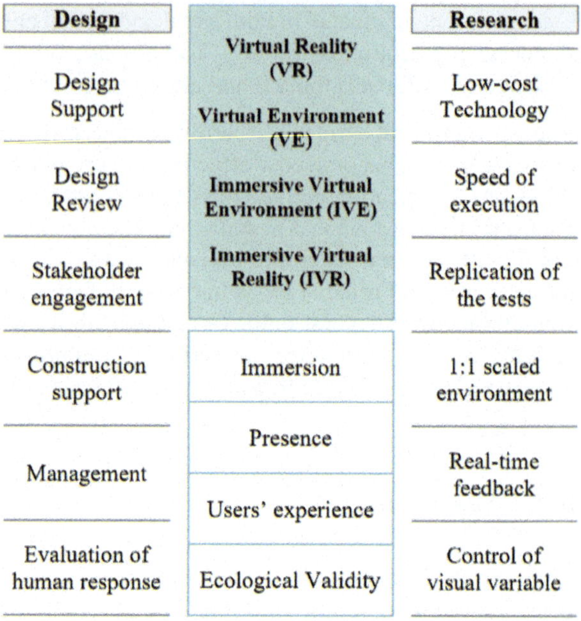

Fig. 3.1 Advantages and concepts of VR in building design and occupant research sectors

These new technologies are low-cost, and have lots of benefits, in terms of speed of execution and replication of tests. It allows the users to be immersed in a 1:1 scaled environment, while researchers and designers collect real-time feedback, measure end-user behaviour and easily control the design variables [10].

Moreover, users can experience the so-called Acoustic Virtual Reality (AVR) [11], if Virtual Reality is combined with acoustical stimuli, or mixed-Immersive Virtual Environment (mIVE) [12] if the Virtual Environment is combined with a climatic chamber generating thermal stimuli. Consequently, by simulating actual building spaces and visual elements, Virtual Reality can be adopted to achieve effective evidence-based design, proving its reliability in scientific experiments (Fig. 3.1).

3.3 The Evolution of VR in Building Occupants Research

The widespread use of Virtual Reality technology has resulted in studies actively evaluating and verifying its utility and applicability to Building Occupants Research. In this context, Fig. 3.2 shows a bar chart about the evolution of the number of scientific papers published over the last two decades (the chart is based on the Scopus database of 2.613 publications). It is evident how increasingly the volume of VR-based scientific documents continues to rise each year, with various contributions from researchers around the world. This evolution reflects the increasing recognition of Virtual Reality and Immersive Virtual Environments as powerful tools with a huge

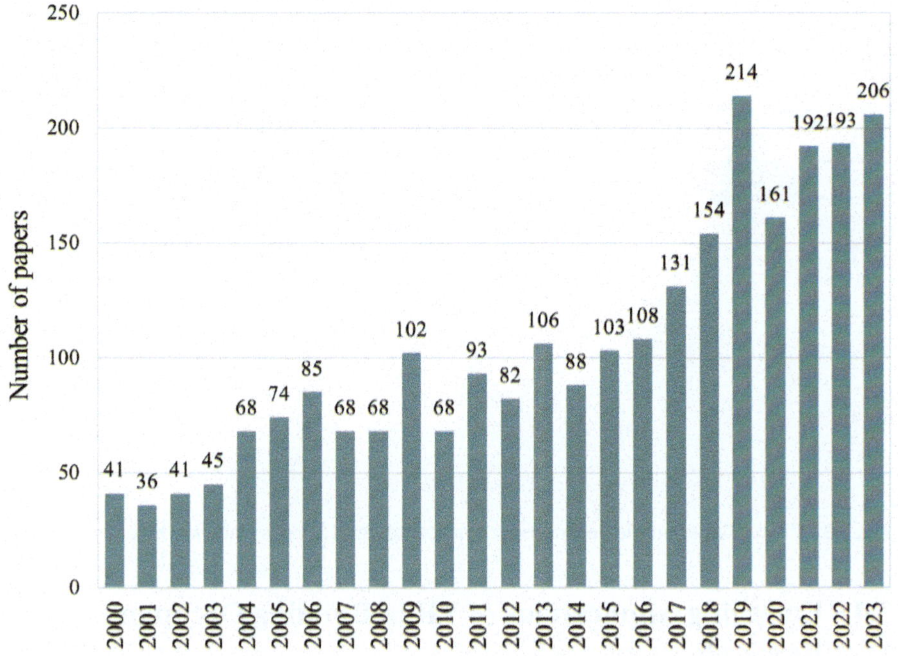

Fig. 3.2 Evolution by year of the VR-related scientific paper production according to Scopus Database with TITLE-ABS-KEY ("virtual reality" OR "immersive virtual environment" AND "building" AND "comfort" OR "work" OR "behaviour")

promise to revolutionise the Building Occupants Research field while enhancing users' experiences.

Virtual Reality literature has also a relevant variability across countries which reflects the dynamic nature of this research field (Fig. 3.3). In the early years (2000–2005-year range), research efforts were concentrated in countries like the United States and the United Kingdom nations where ground-breaking work paved the way for further studies. Later, the advancements in technology have enabled a worldwide spreading interest in Virtual Reality. Since it has become more accessible and affordable, more countries beginning to contribute significantly to the literature, such as China and Germany (2005–2010-year range). In the last decade (2015–2024) also Italy has become part of the top five nations with more publications, particularly ranking third after the United States and China since 2020.

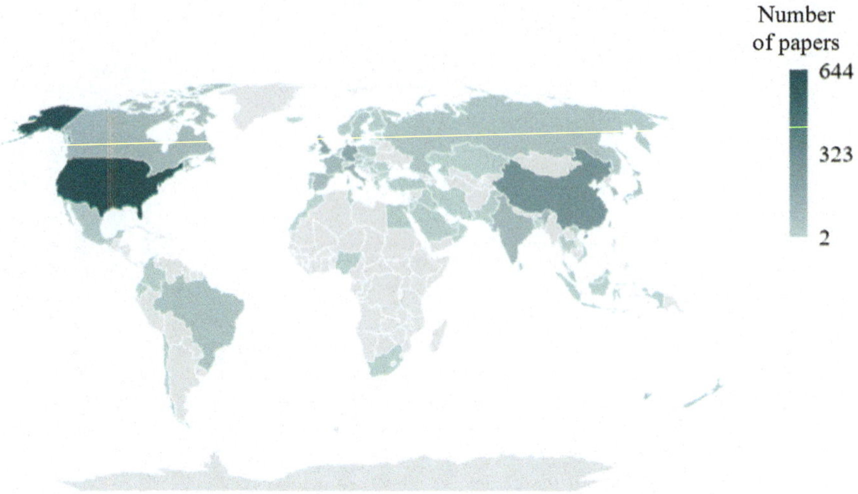

Fig. 3.3 VR-related scientific paper production according to Scopus Database by country

3.4 Emerging Applications of VR in Building Occupants Research

Researchers have argued that Virtual Reality may support innovative activities by allowing experimentation in-depth and the involvement of all in the innovation process [13]. That is why Virtual Environments are demonstrating their potential in data collection and examination in the multidisciplinary Architectural, Engineering and Construction fields. Despite that, VR is still a newly emerging technology at the beginning stages of exploration for scientific research in building occupant research.

Recently, the widespread use of this technology has resulted in studies actively evaluating and verifying its utility and applicability to Building Occupants Research.

A significant barrier to empower the adoption of these tools is the *limited amount of "validation" studies*. The aim is to confirm the effectiveness and accuracy of Virtual Environments in the representation and comparison to real-life scenarios, simulating indoor environmental stimuli and their influence on users. These validation efforts can enhance the reliability and applicability of VR in studying human-building interactions.

To the best of the author's knowledge, only a few experiments validated VEs on Building Occupants Research through the comparison with their real counterparts. Overall, the adequacy of Virtual Environments in replicating physical settings was assessed by looking for the reliability of the collected data concerning thermal and visual comfort, tasks related to work efficiency, occupants' perceptions and physiological parameters. Fewer attempts of validation concerned the thermal and lighting behaviour of individuals. Single-domain research is the most widespread study design type in validation processes. Namely, researchers assess the potential of VR to adequately replicate the effect of indoor environmental conditions on occupants' experience. The majority of those studies did not consider environmental conditions variations, thus RE and IVE were compared in the same controlled conditions (e.g., equal indoor temperature, light settings). Few multi-domain validation studies were carried out by combining more than one environmental stimulus (independent variables), such as thermal and visual stimuli and additionally assessing the cross-modal effect of the thermal domain on visual response. In most cases, the differences in results between the virtual and real environments were not significant providing evidence that IVEs can be effective tools to support and understand building occupant research.

On the other side, one of the most common applications of Virtual Reality in this field is the standalone simulation of indoor environments, without a real counterpart, and evaluation of VR suitability via questionnaires asking participants to self-report their sense of presence and immersivity and cybersickness disorders.

In this context, a wide range of studies addressed single-domain research considering, for instance, the influence of different artificial and natural lighting statuses, correlated colour temperature, viewing location or façade characteristics (i.e., window-to-wall ratio, outside view) and indoor settings (i.e., green elements and layout variations). Multi-domain approaches remain still in part understudied with a limited number of studies combining thermal-visual stimuli. Additionally, few studies addressed crossed-modal effects considering the effect of visual condition (e.g., colour) on thermal comfort and vice versa, and the effect of acoustics on thermal and visual comfort.

In general, VR settings are commonly adopted to facilitate the investigation of the effect of indoor environmental conditions on building occupants. Both validation and standalone studies focus on the perceptual responses of individuals, followed by task accuracy and cognitive functions, physiological measures and behavioural analysis on lighting settings and thermal comfort (dependent variables).

3.5 Data Collection Methods

In Building Occupants Research, Virtual Reality applications offer a versatile and powerful tool for studying indoor environments and measuring human factors. To ensure the reliability and validity of the research outcomes, it is essential to discuss how the investigated dependent variables are collected during these experiments since they express individuals' responses to variations of the independent variables (i.e., the investigated stimuli) [14].

The most common evaluation metric in this research domain involves *subjective approaches*, such as surveys, interviews, or observations to gather feedback directly from participants about their perceptions, preferences, comfort levels, and behaviour. *Users' comfort* is typically assessed by self-reported perception according to well-established standards, such as the standards ISO 10551:2019 [15] and ANSI/

ASHRAE 55:2004 [16] for sensation, preference and comfort ratings, ISO 12913-2: 2018 [17] and ITU-R BS 1116-3: 2015 [18] for the acoustical field-study. *Perceptions* are evaluated through questionnaires depending on the dependent variable of interest, concerning, for instance, the sense of privacy, visual comfort, aesthetic assessment, sense of inner space and openness. The *emotional state* is typically investigated using standardized scales widely used in psychology research, such as the Positive and Negative Affect Schedule (PANAS), Visual Analogue Scale (VAS) and the Self-assessment manikin Questionnaire (SAM), while the State-Trait Anxiety Inventory (STAI) often adopted for stress responses.

In addition to subjective assessment methods, some studies collected *objective measures. Physiological responses* of individuals in IVEs are typically collected to be correlated with individuals' perceptions. In particular, heart rate, electrodermal activity or skin conductance, blood pressure and skin temperature are the most collected data with wearable devices. Such metrics are adopted as an indicator of psychological and physiological arousal and to assess stress [19] due to their sensitivity to the activation of the sympathetic nerve in response to psychological stimuli. Indeed, when a stimulus (e.g., an object, a person, a situation) is perceived as personally significant, a subject experiences an increase in stress level or emotional arousal, the brain sends a signal through the sympathetic nerve activating the eccrine sweat glands promoting the sudomotor, increasing heart rate or decreasing the peripheral circulation causing a reduction in skin temperature. For instance, this usually happens in the presence of negative emotions (e.g., anger, sadness, fear) and stress load. On the contrary, higher skin temperature values, lower pulse rate and sweat gland measures indicated a more relaxed status. In addition, neurophysiological responses using Electroencephalography and eye-tracking data are also collected. In particular, involuntary eye-movement metrics, such as blinking, pupil diameter, fixations and saccades, are adopted as a measure of cognitive load. Indeed, during cognitive-demanding tasks, emotional arousal and engagement in a scene, pupils tend to dilate, eye blinks tend to be inhibited, number and duration of fixations tend to increase.

In addition to physiological responses, some studies investigated also individuals' *work efficiency or productivity*, through reading tasks which are common obligations for daily office work. Only a few studies focused on *cognitive functions* which are important across different tasks and can be investigated using tests related to several mental abilities, including attention, mental flexibility, comprehension, creativity, and working memory. Attention is an indicator of the ability to quickly focus on relevant stimuli within the environment. It has been categorized into two main components: sustained attention and executive attention. Sustained attention refers to the ability to internally maintain control in the absence of significant external stimuli. Conversely, executive attention involves the allocation of attentional resources to goal-directed tasks and the inhibition of irrelevant information [20]. In particular, executive attention implies more specific cognitive processes such as cognitive flexibility and inhibitory control. Working memory is a cognitive system responsible for the temporary storage and manipulation of information necessary for complex cognitive tasks, while creativity, is the capacity to generate novel and valuable ideas, providing insights into divergent thinking abilities [21]. Finally, comprehension is the cognitive process of extracting meaning from information received through language or reading modalities, involving critical thinking to interpret relationships and integrate information. Sometimes these tests are combined with subjective measures asking users to estimate their task fatigue and *workload stress* while performing cognitive tests, such as the NASA-Task Load Index (TLX) questionnaire. Overall, tasks to assess work efficiency are presented with different methods, e.g., on the virtual computer monitor on virtual papers, slides or via headphones.

Furthermore, to understand the influence of preliminary design decisions on *occupants' behaviour*, few experiments in IVE addressed the complexity of the human-building interaction domain. The main attention is directed towards blinds and lighting adjustment with limited monitoring of participants' interaction with climatic systems (e.g., heater, fans, air conditioning) to achieve better indoor thermal comfort. Concerning the investigation of the human-building interaction and adaptive behavioural assessment, the Theory of Planned Behaviour [22] is often employed to subjectively measure respondents' awareness of consequences, attitudes toward reducing energy use, knowledge about the energy consumption of electric appliances and perceived behavioural control. According to this theory developed by Ajzen et al. [22], human behaviour is driven by behavioural beliefs about behaviour consequences, normative beliefs about the expectation of others over the users' behaviour, and control beliefs related to the presence of factors that may facilitate or limit a behaviour. Behavioural beliefs result in a favourable or unfavourable attitude toward the behaviour, normative beliefs in a perceived social pressure or subjective norm, while control beliefs determine perceived behavioural control. As a result, their combination leads the users to a behavioural intention. In particular, the more favourable the attitude, the less social pressure, and the greater perceived control, the greater will be the users' intention to perform a behaviour which will be finalised (turning into a behaviour) in the presence of an opportunity and sufficient control.

As a result, combining subjective and objective measures (Fig. 3.4) in VR-based studies provides a comprehensive understanding of building occupants' responses to the variation of indoor environmental conditions with great potential to inform evidence-based design practices.

3.6 Challenges

Recent advancements in Virtual Reality technology offer a unique opportunity to support and expand the research in the built environment as properly designed indoor spaces are vital components for living and working. The overall aim is to discover, through the VR tool, the relationships among the changes and characteristics of the indoor spaces, in terms of layout (windows size, walls and light colour) and stimuli (thermal, visual, acoustical), with users' comfort and perceptions, productivity and adaptive behaviour.

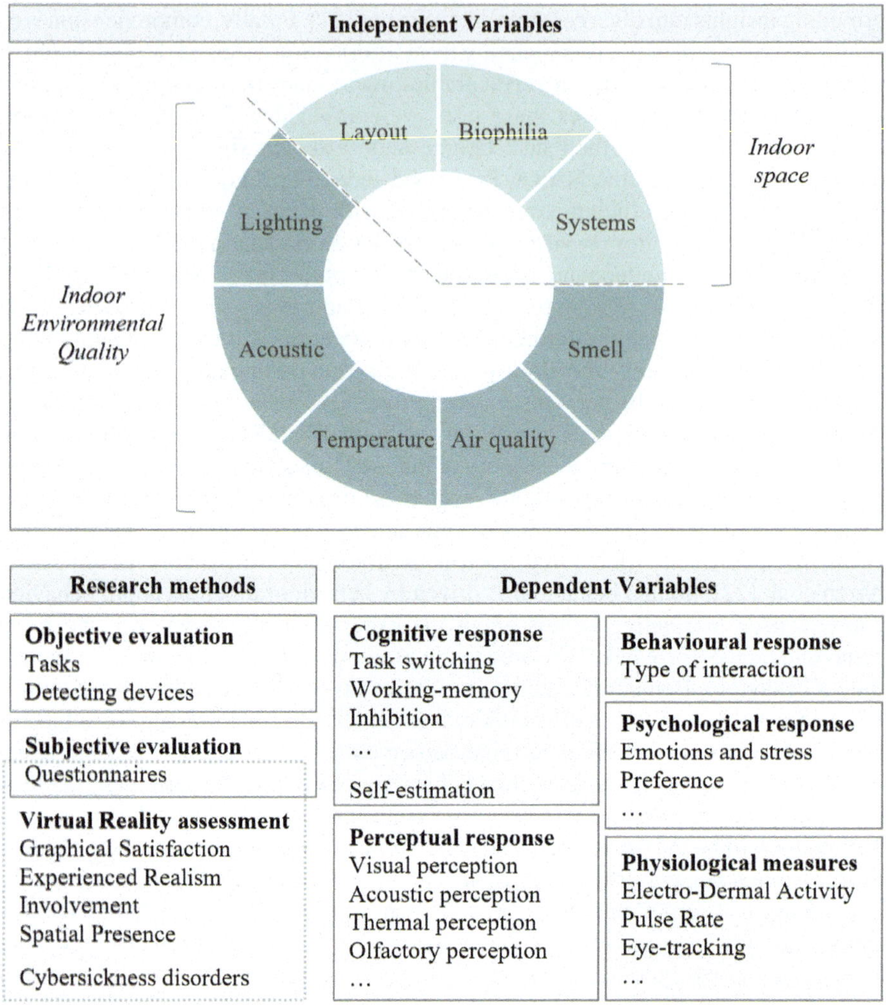

Fig. 3.4 Scheme of research strategies considering independent variables, research methods and dependent variables

Despite the rapidly growing trend and the benefits of using Virtual Reality, several challenges limit its adoption to advance the field of multisensory Building Occupants Research and enhance design guidelines and user-centred systems:

- the difficulty in using this technology lies in obtaining valid, reproducible, and generalizable research findings from virtual to real environments, thus requiring more research attention and validation efforts to enhance the reliability and effectiveness of collected data and related outcomes.

- The majority of studies adopted Virtual Environments in isolation, lacking a comparison with real counterparts, and inconsistently analysing users' sense of presence and immersivity and cybersickness disorders to support the suitability of the tool.
- VR-based validations and standalone studies focus on single-domain investigations with a limited amount of multi-domain experiments on thermal and visual stimuli, neglecting acoustic settings, for instance.
- IVE-based experiments have been effectively carried out to study primarily the influence of visual domain and indoor layout variations on individuals' subjective and objective measures. A possible explanation is that virtual settings facilitate the modification of the visual dimension with reduced time and cost efforts (e.g., artificial and natural lighting statuses, illuminance level, and colour temperature are one-click update metrics).
- Limited attention is given to adaptive behaviour investigations concerning the thermal settings (e.g., thermostat and air conditioning adjustment) and a comprehensive assessment of human cognitive functions.
- In the process of evaluating the perception of the environment and psychological aspects, a crucial gap is the inhomogeneous approach to the administration of the survey which influences outcomes reliability. Most of the studies administrated questionnaires at the end of the experimental phase, after the removal of the head-mounted display, leading to not fully realistic perceptions because the ratings of the virtual environment are given in the real world. In other cases, surveys are provided verbally to participants during the experiment session, thus potentially disrupting the immersion level throughout the tests. Therefore, it is crucial to create a seamless transition between the virtual experience and the questionnaire to guarantee that the information collected is trustworthy while maintaining immersion and a sense of presence throughout the experiment.
- The study samples were typically limited in size and were homogenous resulting in a lack of diversity and representativeness of the entire population, thereby limiting the generalizability of the outcomes.
- A key challenge preventing VR from becoming more widespread in evidence-based indoor design practises to foster occupants' work efficiency, comfort, and behaviour, is the lack of an established protocol for conducting rigorous experiments in virtual settings. This lack of consistency could be translated into a critical weakness in building standards criteria which currently do not include evidence-based outcomes established by VR experiments.

References

1. Council National Research, Funding a Revolution: Government support for computing research, 1999. https://doi.org/10.17226/6323

2. M.A. Muhanna, Virtual reality and the CAVE: Taxonomy, interaction challenges and research directions, J. King Saud Univ. - Comput. Inf. Sci. 27 (2015) 344–361. https://doi.org/10.1016/j.jksuci.2014.03.023
3. M. Mollazadeh, Y. Zhu, Application of virtual environments for biophilic design: A critical review, Buildings. 11 (2021). https://doi.org/10.3390/buildings11040148
4. H. Alamirah, M. Schweiker, E. Azar, Immersive virtual environments for occupant comfort and adaptive behavior research – A comprehensive review of tools and applications, Build. Environ. 207 (2022). https://doi.org/10.1016/j.buildenv.2021.108396
5. P. Caserman, A. Garcia-Agundez, A. Gámez Zerban, S. Göbel, Cybersickness in current-generation virtual reality head-mounted displays: systematic review and outlook, Virtual Real. 25 (2021) 1153–1170. https://doi.org/10.1007/s10055-021-00513-6
6. Y. Zhang, H. Liu, S.C. Kang, M. Al-Hussein, Virtual reality applications for the built environment: Research trends and opportunities, Autom. Constr. 118 (2020) 103311. https://doi.org/10.1016/j.autcon.2020.103311.
7. J.M. Davila Delgado, L. Oyedele, P. Demian, T. Beach, A research agenda for augmented and virtual reality in architecture, engineering and construction, Adv. Eng. Informatics. 45 (2020) 101122. https://doi.org/10.1016/j.aei.2020.101122.
8. Y. Chen, Z. Cui, L. Hao, Virtual reality in lighting research: Comparing physical and virtual lighting environments, Light. Res. Technol. 51 (2019) 820–837. https://doi.org/10.1177/1477153518825387.
9. H.I. Jo, J.Y. Jeon, Perception of urban soundscape and landscape using different visual environment reproduction methods in virtual reality, Appl. Acoust. 186 (2022) 108498. https://doi.org/10.1016/j.apacoust.2021.108498.
10. Heydarian, J.P. Carneiro, D. Gerber, B. Becerik-Gerber, T. Hayes, W. Wood, Immersive virtual environments versus physical built environments: A benchmarking study for building design and user-built environment explorations, Autom. Constr. 54 (2015) 116–126. https://doi.org/10.1016/j.autcon.2015.03.020.
11. F. Pind, C. Jeong, H.S. Llopis, K. Kosikowski, J. Strømann-andersen, Acoustic Virtual Reality – Methods and challenges, Balt. Acoust. Meet. (2018) 1–11.
12. S. Saeidi, G. Rentala, T. Rizzuto, T. Hong, N. Johannsen, Y. Zhu, Exploring thermal state in mixed immersive virtual environments, J. Build. Eng. 44 (2021) 102918. https://doi.org/10.1016/j.jobe.2021.102918.
13. J. Whyte, Virtual Reality and the Built Environment, 2002.
14. G. Chinazzo, R.K. Andersen, E. Azar, V.M. Barthelmes, C. Becchio, L. Belussi, C. Berger, S. Carlucci, S.P. Corgnati, S. Crosby, L. Danza, L. de Castro, M. Favero, S. Gauthier, R.T. Hellwig, Q. Jin, J. Kim, M. Sarey Khanie, D. Khovalyg, C. Lingua, A. Luna-Navarro, A. Mahdavi, C. Miller, I. Mino-Rodriguez, I. Pigliautile, A.L. Pisello, R.F. Rupp, A.-M. Sadick, F. Salamone, M. Schweiker, M. Syndicus, G. Spigliantini, N.G. Vasquez, D. Vakalis, M. Vellei, S. Wei, Quality criteria for multi-domain studies in the indoor environment: Critical review towards research guidelines and recommendations, Build. Environ. 226 (2022) 109719. https://doi.org/10.1016/j.buildenv.2022.109719.
15. ISO - International Organization for Standardization, ISO 10551:2019 Ergonomics of the physical environment -- Subjective judgement scales for assessing physical environments, (2019).
16. ASHRAE Standard, ANSI/ASHRAE Standard 55–2004: Thermal Environmental Conditions for Human Occupancy, Am. Soc. Heating, Refrig. Air-Conditioning Eng. Inc. 2004 (2004) 1–34.
17. ISO - International Organization for Standardization, ISO 12913–1:2014 Acoustics — Soundscape — Part 1: Definition and conceptual framework, (2014).
18. ITU-R BS.1116-3, Methods for the subjective assessment of small impairments in audio systems BS Series Broadcasting service (sound), Int. Telecommun. Union. 3 (2015).
19. M. Awada, B. Becerik-Gerber, R. Liu, M. Seyedrezaei, Z. Lu, M. Xenakis, G. Lucas, S.C. Roll, S. Narayanan, Ten questions concerning the impact of environmental stress on office workers, Build. Environ. 229 (2023) 109964. https://doi.org/10.1016/j.buildenv.2022.109964.

20. L.A. Sharam, K.M. Mayer, O. Baumann, Design by nature : The influence of windows on cognitive performance and affect, J. Environ. Psychol. 85 (2023) 101923. https://doi.org/10.1016/j.jenvp.2022.101923.
21. J.P. Guilford, Creativity: Yesterday, today, and tomorrow, J. Creat. Behav. 1 (1967) 3–14. https://doi.org/10.1002/j.2162-6057.1967.tb00002.x.
22. Ajzen, The theory of planned behaviour, Organ. Behav. Hum. Decis. Process. 50 (1991) 179–211. https://doi.org/10.1080/10410236.2018.1493416

Chapter 4
Definition of Framework and Guidelines for IVR Applications

Abstract Despite a growing interest in VR-based study to support Building Occupants Research, the development of a mature and holistic science of Human-Centric indoor environments is still impeded by the lack of an agreed-upon conceptual framework. Concerning the need and relevance of a strict measure protocol, a comprehensive experimental framework is presented to organize and enhance the application of VR in building occupant research. The proposed experimental framework establishes pre- and post-trials procedures, based on well-known validation types of the research study (i.e., internal and external validity) and measurements (i.e., content, face and criterion validity). The former allows a strict experimental design to produce trustworthy data, the latter to organize the measurements, correlate the results with existing studies, and make general conclusions looking for a cause-effect relationship between variables. Practical suggestions for researchers are then provided.

4.1 Study Set-Up

In the early research design stage, the definition of dependent and independent variable variables is guided by the research objectives.

To ensure reliable and valid results, the comprehensive coverage and measurement of all contents of the constructs is necessary. As an initial step, research should consider whether a specific content (e.g., test, survey) measures what it is intended to measure (i.e., the construct of interest) [1]. Those contents should be selected based on existing well-established literature, standards, and theories.

Selected instruments serve as indicators of the intended constructs: the more they represent the dependent variables, the greater the ***Content Validity*** of the study [2].

Hereunder, are presented practical suggestions to be adopted during the pre-experimental phase.

Productivity may be assessed with objective measures by analysing the three most domain-general cognitive functions that are important across a variety of daily working tasks [3–5]: “working memory”, which refers to the ability to keep information in mind and manipulate it, “inhibition”, which refers to the ability to control

A. Latini, *Immersive Virtual Reality for a Building Occupant-Centric Design*, Digital Innovations in Architecture, Engineering and Construction,
https://doi.org/10.1007/978-3-031-66028-3_4

attention and prevail impulses, and "task switching", which refers to the ability to flexibly switch from one activity to another in a very short-time. Workers' self-estimation of productivity level can be also coupled with objective assessment methods, even if their suitability is widely recognised and adopted in long-term real-settings studies.

Self-reports should explore each construct indicator, such as sensation, evaluation, and preference for comfort; spatial presence, graphical satisfaction, realism, and involvement for the sense of presence and immersivity factors; disorders for the cybersickness measure. The proper number of items should be selected to deal also with the time constraint of Virtual Reality exposure. The researcher might need to screen and revise the questions while developing a reliable, effective and complete investigation tool coherent with the research purpose. Additionally, questionnaires should collect individuals' demographics, such as gender, age, and educational level, which may be confounding variables and explain some cause-effect relationships in the outcomes.

Subsequently, a strict experimental design is needed to support the ***Internal Validity*** establishing the extent to which an effect found in a study can be taken to be genuinely caused by manipulation of the independent variable [1].

Specifically, a biased sample is the most crucial threat to Internal Validity. Researchers can carry out a "repeated-measures" or "independent-measure" design research having the same group of individuals performing all the treatment conditions or having a different group in each treatment condition, respectively. A mix of those two can also be carried out with participants exposed to all conditions of one independent variable and to some of the conditions of another independent variable. To overcome the inner drawbacks of each experimental procedure since the early research design phase, it is necessary to counterbalance time-related factors, order effect, individual differences and other biases that can be a threat to internal validity [6]. For instance, the order presentation of the test, surveys and treatment conditions needs to be randomised. The sample should be well-balanced in terms of gender and demographics to enable the generalisation of the results. Due to its relevant effect on the results, the sample size should be also adequate and determined a-priori by carrying out a power analysis to ensure its adequacy in detecting significant effects based on the statistical power and the effect size.

Before the experimental session begins, a pilot study can be carried out to assess the Content and Internal Validity of the experiment by screening any potential problems linked to the research instruments and protocol, thus achieving ***Face Validity***.

After the definition of all the crucial aspects of the experimental design from a theoretical point of view (Content, Internal, and Face Validity) and participants' recruitment, the experimental sessions take place.

Before the empirical data analysis, an intermediate step involves ***external-Ecological Validity*** which refers to the ability of Virtual Reality to properly represent real settings and environments. Specifically, it demands a high level of immersion achievable through an effective virtual model development and the self-reports about the sense of presence, immersivity and cybersickness disorders should be properly analysed.

Indeed, it is suggested *to create an extremely detailed model*, in terms of objects, materials and light representation, to be experienced through a suitable head-mounted display concerning the resolution image per eye.

Questionnaires need to be integrated and administrated within the virtual model to ensure a fully immersive experience and then reliable data. Since participants provide feedback directly about the virtual environment when exposed to it, authors will be allowed to avoid "break-in-presence" [7] which can threaten the Ecological Validity. *Cybersickness, sense of presence and immersivity* need to be investigated to properly assess the virtual environment and support the Content Validity according to well-established surveys, such as the Virtual Reality Sickness Questionnaire, Igroup Presence Questionnaires and Slater-Usoh-Steed. The latter can be combined to analyse four attributes on Likert scales (from "totally disagree" to "totally agree"): Graphical Satisfaction, Spatial Presence, Involvement, and Experienced Realism within the virtual environment.

To verify the Ecological Validity, the author suggests: *comparing the average value of each indicator to previous literature studies* that used the same evaluation instrument and ensuring that scores are at least *equal or higher than a moderate-high level* (e.g., 4 on a five-point scale) which means detecting a good level of sense of presence and immersivity. In addition, it is necessary for the majority of *the subjects not to have experienced high disorder levels* (e.g., general discomfort, fatigue, eye strain, difficulty in focusing, headache, vertigo).

Lastly, *limiting the virtual exposure time to 25/30 min* mitigates the occurrence of any disturbances that could invalidate the test due to discomforting participants [8–10]. It is suggested to include in the experimental schedule, after the introduction of participants in the virtual environment, 30 s of *rest with eyes closed* to reduce any psychological fluctuations related to the Virtual Environment exposure, and 3/4 min of *virtual scene adaptation* to facilitate visual and acoustical immersion, for instance [11].

Researchers should be aware that VR-induced symptoms are a recurrent issue in VR experiments and might depend on poor virtual experiments [12], the quality of hardware (HMD characteristics) and personal susceptibility to motion sickness which can be investigated in a pre-experimental survey [10]. However, longer exposure time can be adopted but researchers should be concerned about any subsequent related to potential high disorder levels. A possible solution could be the split of long-term experiments into shorter test sessions providing a break between different experimental treatments, for instance. In any case, researchers should avoid the removal of the head-mounted display in order not to negatively disrupt participants' immersivity.

4.2 Study Conduction (Data Collection)

Following the study set-up based on the research objective and hypothesis, data are collected within *experimental activities*. Experimental settings and procedures play a fundamental role in ensuring the reliability of outcomes.

In general, it is imperative to clearly define the conditions to which participants are exposed, including the *type of independent variables*, and *exposure time*, to allow the replicability of the experiments and the monitoring of possible confounding variables.

At a global level, all the dependent variables are investigated during the study conduction in line with the Content Validity and based on a rigorous experimental schedule and design. For instance, in assessing work efficiency, cognitive tests are administered, behavioural interaction with building systems is recorded, while comfort, immersivity and cybersickness construct are investigated during the post-experimental phase following an adequate exposure time to stimuli. Additionally, besides the independent variable or stimuli selected, it is important to measure and report all the environmental stimuli, even additional factors that can be potentially relevant acting as confounders. Therefore, at a local level, environmental and physiological measures can be implemented to understand the interaction underlying a specific environmental exposure–response relationship.

An overview of variables that can be potentially collected for Building Occupant Research at each stage of the experimental protocol is depicted in Fig. 4.1.

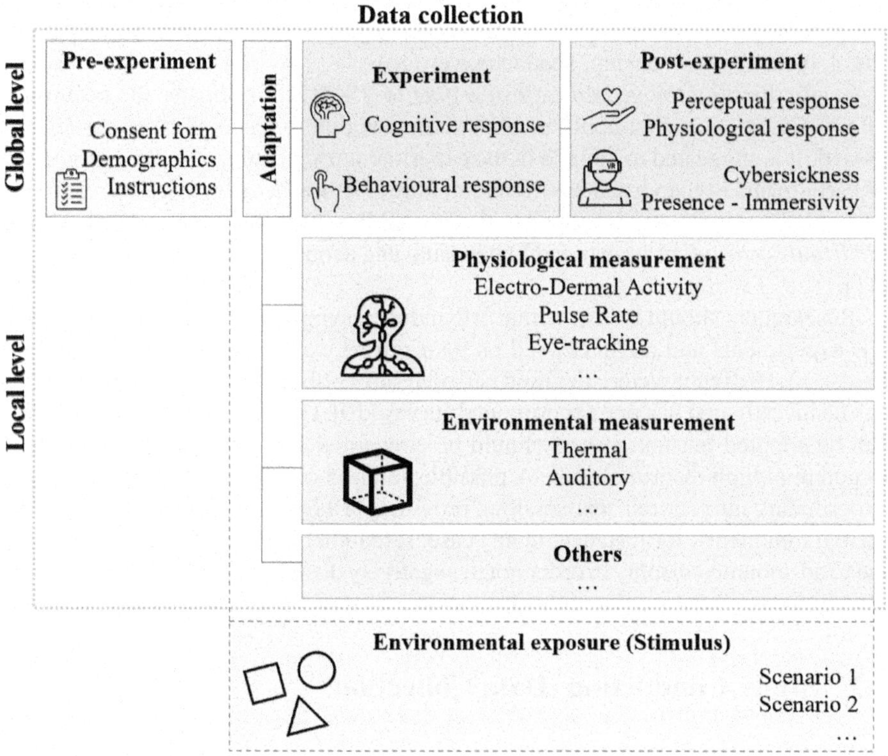

Fig. 4.1 Overview of the collected data during an experimental phase and structure of research activities

4.3 Study Analysis (Data Insight)

This section does not focus on how to analyse data but rather on establishing the ***Criterion-concurrent Validity***, which refers to the extent to which test results align with those on another test intended to measure the same construct [1].

After the trials, once Ecological Validity is confirmed, the procedure involves the comparison with currently existing measures of the construct. In particular, in VR validation studies, the objective is to examine the adequacy of replicating real-world situations and the reliability of the technology. Consequently, the outcomes of various constructs (e.g., comfort levels, task performance, behavioural responses, physiological parameters) need to be compared between the two procedures, namely the real and the virtual environment. Otherwise, the results of VR standalone studies can be compared to the ones from previous research activities using similar measurement methods, that have already been validated [13]. The overall objective may be looking to data insight about the influence of environmental stimulus on individuals' responses and the interaction underlying a cause-effect relationship. For example, when examining the correlation between thermal comfort and adaptive behaviour, it is expected that the higher the indoor air temperature in a room, the more participants will report a higher thermal sensation and discomfort levels leading to a desirable interaction with building systems. Similarly, in the context of acoustics, the greater the noise annoyance the lower the task accuracy. If the tool (Virtual Reality) performs well, a high correlation should be discovered in terms of variables' behaviour or cause-effect relationships (Fig. 4.2).

The fundamental steps of the developed framework to be included in the research design supporting and facilitating the conduction of studies in effective, reliable and valid virtual environments are summarised in Fig. 4.3.

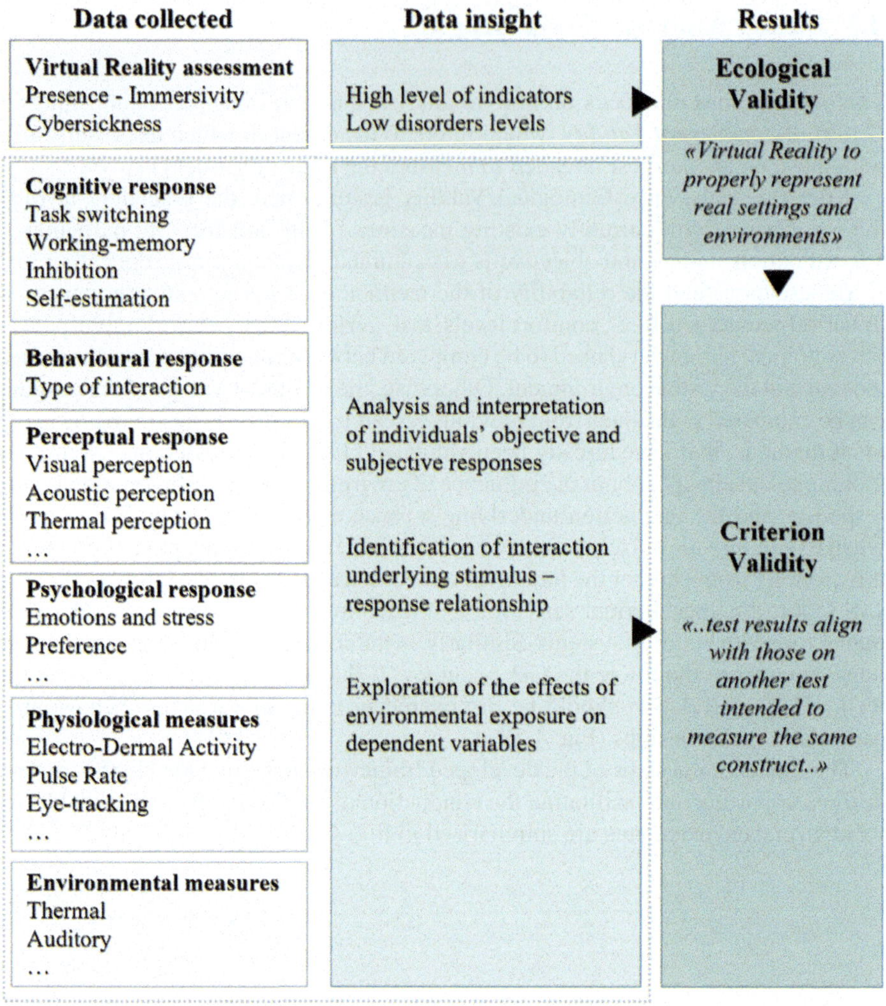

Fig. 4.2 Overview of data insight and results concerning the ecological and criterion validity

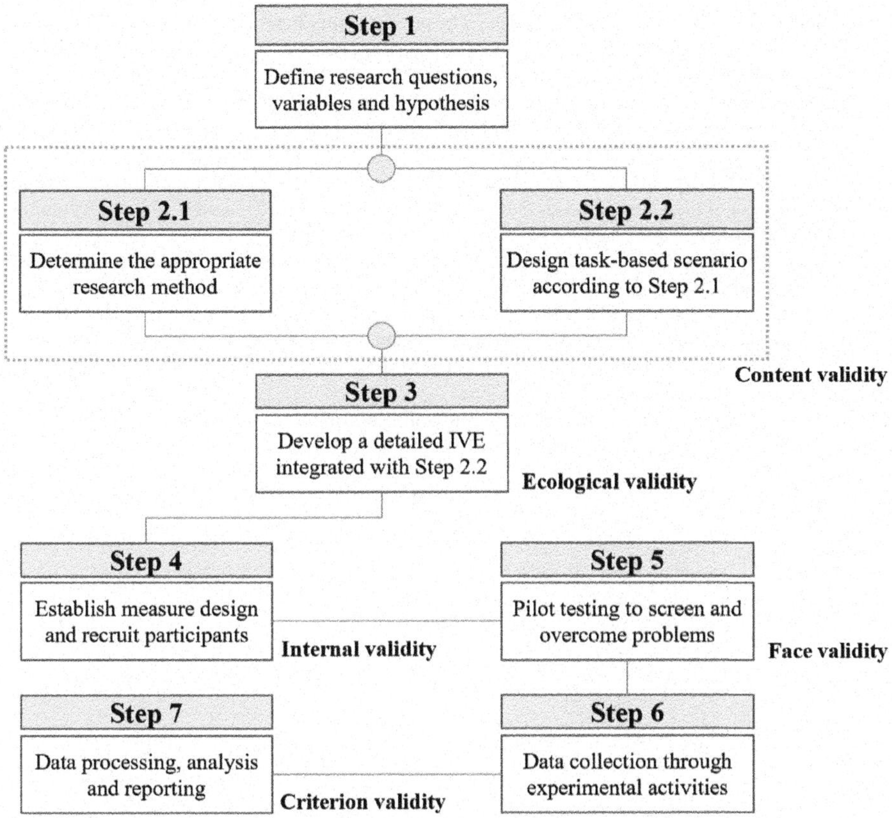

Fig. 4.3 Approach to include the developed framework and conduct research in Immersive Virtual Environments (IVE)

References

1. H. Coolican, Research Methods and Statistics in Psychology, 2018. https://doi.org/10.4324/9781315201009.
2. H.K. Mohajan, Two Criteria for Good Measurements in Research: Validity and Reliability, Ann. Spiru Haret Univ. 17 (2017) 59–82. https://doi.org/10.26458/1746.
3. Miyake, N.P. Friedman, M.J. Emerson, A.H. Witzki, A. Howerter, T.D. Wager, The Unity and Diversity of Executive Functions and Their Contributions to Complex "Frontal Lobe" Tasks: A Latent Variable Analysis, Cogn. Psychol. 41 (2000) 49–100. https://doi.org/10.1006/cogp.1999.0734.
4. Diamond, Executive functions, Annu. Rev. Psychol. 64 (2013) 135–168. https://doi.org/10.1146/annurev-psych-113011-143750.
5. ASHRAE Standard, Journal - June 2019, 61 (2019) 1–85.
6. F.J.L.-A.B.F. GRAVETTER, Research Method for Behavioural Science, 2012.
7. H. Alamirah, M. Schweiker, E. Azar, Immersive virtual environments for occupant comfort and adaptive behavior research – A comprehensive review of tools and applications, Build. Environ. 207 (2021) 108396. https://doi.org/10.1016/j.buildenv.2021.108396.

8. J. Munafo, M. Diedrick, T.A. Stoffregen, The virtual reality head-mounted display Oculus Rift induces motion sickness and is sexist in its effects, Exp. Brain Res. 235 (2017) 889–901. https://doi.org/10.1007/s00221-016-4846-7.
9. Y. Zhu, S. Saeidi, T. Rizzuto, A. Roetzel, R. Kooima, Potential and challenges of immersive virtual environments for occupant energy behavior modeling and validation: A literature review, J. Build. Eng. 19 (2018) 302–319. https://doi.org/10.1016/j.jobe.2018.05.017.
10. Heydarian, B. Becerik-Gerber, Use of immersive virtual environments for occupant behaviour monitoring and data collection, J. Build. Perform. Simul. 10 (2017) 484–498. https://doi.org/10.1080/19401493.2016.1267801.
11. J. Li, Y. Jin, S. Lu, W. Wu, P. Wang, Building environment information and human perceptual feedback collected through a combined virtual reality (VR) and electroencephalogram (EEG) method, Energy Build. 224 (2020) 110259. https://doi.org/10.1016/j.enbuild.2020.110259.
12. S. Saeidi, G. Rentala, T. Rizzuto, T. Hong, N. Johannsen, Y. Zhu, Exploring thermal state in mixed immersive virtual environments, J. Build. Eng. 44 (2021) 102918. https://doi.org/10.1016/j.jobe.2021.102918.
13. J.M. Jones, Validity of nutritional screening and assessment tools, Nutrition. 20 (2004) 312–317. https://doi.org/10.1016/j.nut.2003.11.005.

Chapter 5
Validation of the Framework and IVR

Abstract The use of Virtual Reality to enhance Building Occupant Research is emerging, but validation studies comparing Real and Virtual Environments (RE, IVE) are still limited. This chapter presents an important contribution providing guidelines to answer the validity issue and describing a step-by-step procedure to organize experimental validity studies from the setup of the Real Environment and test room, going through the workflow for the generation of the virtual model at the base empirical studies and the organization of data collection methods suitable to investigate the dependent variables in both the VE and the real counterpart. The overall process necessary to compare the environments and validate Virtual Reality is presented. Results of an illustrative office room example demonstrated the successful validation of the experimental framework and Virtual Reality as a suitable research design tool. The Ecological Validity of Virtual Reality confirms the possibility of achieving an excellent sense of presence and immersivity and low cybersickness disorders in the presence of an effective and realistic Virtual Environment. The absence of significant differences in dependent variables supports the Criterion Validity highlighting the potential of applying Virtual Reality to detect consistent individuals' responses and supporting a user-centred design and multi-domain investigations.

5.1 The Validation Issue

The evaluation of the overall *validity of Virtual Environments* is one of the challenges in adopting Virtual Reality for research and design purposes.

Suitable Immersive Virtual Environments have the potential to create a psychological state in which the users perceive themself as existing within the virtual space. Thus, it is important to systematically evaluate the end-user experience and immersion within a Virtual Environment.

Although Immersive Virtual Environments offer realistic experiences to users, their faithfulness in replicating real-world settings is often a debated aspect not fully addressed within the building occupants' research domain. Those concerns are due to observed discrepancies between Virtual and Real Environments in terms of users'

A. Latini, *Immersive Virtual Reality for a Building Occupant-Centric Design*, Digital Innovations in Architecture, Engineering and Construction,
https://doi.org/10.1007/978-3-031-66028-3_5

responses or sensory input. For instance, Virtual Environments can properly simulate visual and acoustical stimuli. However, they may lack real sensory cues potentially leading to differences in user perception, subsequent responses and behaviour and affecting the ecological validity of research outcomes.

A critical and careful consideration of the level of immersion, realism, and reliability of results achieved in virtual settings is required to address the relevance of the validation issue. Consequently, a *validation process* against real-world observations is suggested as a standard procedure for the effective implementation of Virtual Reality modalities and new methods in the empirical validation of such novel tools and approaches [1].

This approach can be structured in several steps (Fig. 5.1): the setup of a Real Environment the generation of the Immersive Virtual Environment; data collection through experimental studies based on internal, Content and Face validity using the Virtual Environment and the corresponding real one to test all the relevant constructs; the proper analysis of the results to confirm the Ecological and the Criterion Validity the created virtual model.

According to this comprehensive approach, the adequacy of the experimental framework presented in the previous chapter and Immersive Virtual Environments versus real counterparts can be properly assessed. The aim is to verify the suitability of those experimental tools to support empirical studies in Building Occupant Research looking for the reliability of the outcomes. To enhance comprehension and facilitate the adoption of these meaningful guidelines, the structured steps described below are coupled with an illustrative example.

1 Visual stimuli in the real and virtual environment

▶ **Real environment** (RE)	selection and set-up of the experimental real setting
▶ **Virtual Environment** (VE)	creation of the virtual model as faithful replication of real counterpart

2 Data collection (experimental activity)

3 Validation of the experimental framework and VR as proper research tools

▶ **Reported presence and immersivity**	evaluation of perceived presence in the VE
▶ **Reported cybersickness**	evaluation of perceived sickness after using VR headset
▶ **Response accuracy**	evaluation of accuracy in RE and VE across the dependent variables

Fig. 5.1 Illustration of the validation approach

5.2 Setup of the Real Environment

This paragraph and the following ones present several practical tips for carrying out validation studies of virtual environments and enhancing the effectiveness of the research.

The first step is the *meticulous selection and set-up of a test room serving as the Real Environment (RE)* condition which will be replicated by the Virtual Environment. The main criteria for the selection of the experimental space can be the room size, the possibility of high accessibility to enable in-situ measurements and enhanced control over the room furniture to accommodate similar real and virtual scenarios.

Accurately measuring and documenting relevant physical characteristics such as dimensions, layout, lighting, and indoor environmental quality, leads to a better comprehension and replicability of the activity along with the possibility of controlling possible confounding variables.

Careful consideration should be given to the *control of indoor environmental conditions* which is crucial in maintaining consistency and reproducibility across experiments. This may involve regulating factors such as indoor air temperature, air humidity, illuminance, and sound pressure level. For instance, to resemble the desired indoor conditions a proper HVAC system is needed to adjust thermal settings coupled with a *monitoring system* (e.g., air temperature, humidity, velocity probes) to measure and keep stable conditions for each participant. To ensure the reliability of the collected data and results, the same environmental condition must be ensured in both RE and VE. According to the specific recommendations of the domain guidelines, measurements should be taken in the closest location to the user to correctly evaluate the effect of environmental stimuli on participants' responses.

Additionally, *workstations should be strategically equipped* with all the relevant instruments and located to effectively capture accurate users' responses, interactions, and environmental parameters.

Standardized protocols and instructions must be provided to participants across both the real and the virtual settings with the aim of reducing variability drawbacks while ensuring uniform data collection procedures.

For instance, in a real-world experiment carried out by the author, an office-like medium-sized test room was selected. The test room has a width of 5.93 m, a length of 4.38 and a height of 3.00 m. It was set up to replicate an office working environment: the workstation included a computer, a keyboard, a mouse, an indoor microclimate station and typical systems to adjust thermal comfort (i.e., heater, fan, air conditioning, window). The selected viewpoint (blue point in Fig. 5.2) for participants in the real room matched the position in the virtual scene to enable the comparison between the two environments. Indoor climatic conditions were kept constant and monitored throughout the test sessions to ensure data consistency across the Real and the Virtual Environments. In the illustrative case study, the indoor climatic conditions were on average equal to 24.10 ± 0.26 °C and 24.35 ± 0.32 °C, respectively. As a result, no relevant differences were measured across the experimental sessions that

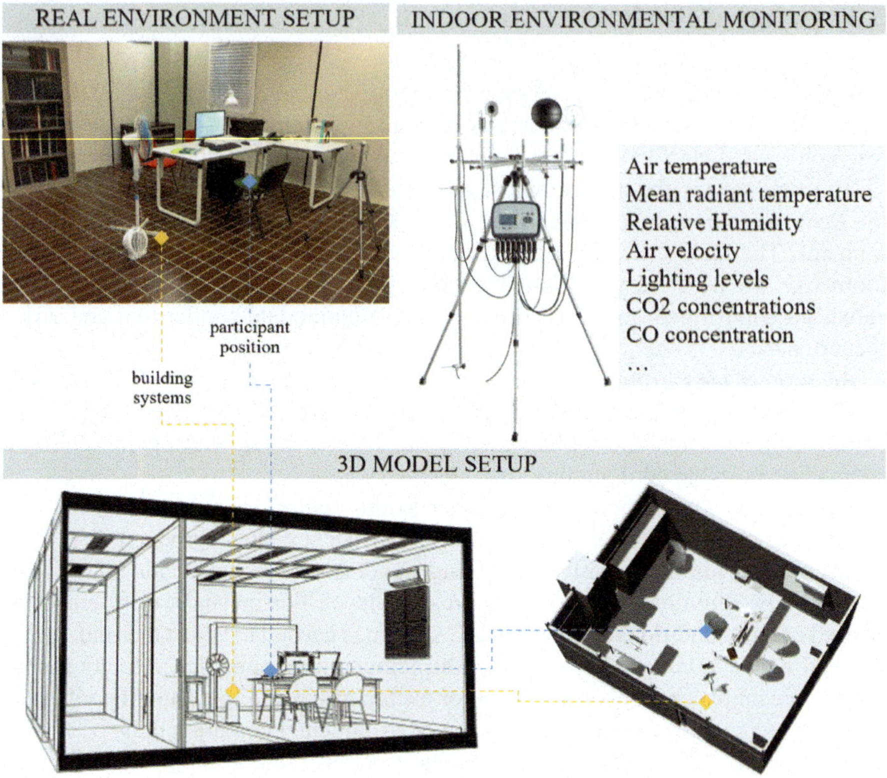

Fig. 5.2 Photogram of the illustrative example: the test room corresponding to the real environment, the monitoring system, and the 3D model at the basis of the virtual environment development

could potentially harm the validation of the model from a thermoception point of view.

Overall, these practical tips have the potential to support researchers in the optimization of the research design, the setup of the Real Environment test room, and facilitating the validation process against virtual environments.

5.3 Generation of the Virtual Environment

To ensure an effective validation process, the Virtual Environment must mimic the key features of its real counterpart to facilitate meaningful and reliable comparisons.

Several practical tips can be adopted when developing through advanced software and modelling techniques a virtual environment faithfully replicating the real-world.

First of all, special attention should be given to *details* ensuring that *the virtual model accurately reflects the physical attributes and characteristics of the Real Environment*. Thus, data about the Real Environment must be comprehensively gathered including dimensions, layout, architectural features, materials, textures, colours, lighting conditions, and other relevant parameters which serve as the basis for the 3D model.

In this context, to increase the model realism, the physical properties of surface materials should be correctly represented. This involves collecting data concerning the reflective properties.

For instance, in the illustrative case study the luminance parameter (L*) and chromatic components (a*, b*) of the CIELab model were extracted using a spectrophotometer (Fig. 5.3). Specifically, for each surface of the physical room (e.g., floor tiles, walls, desks, chairs) several measurements were carried out.

The resulting L*a*b* parameters were mediated and then converted into Red–Green–Blue coordinates to be adopted as one of the virtual model inputs.

Accurately capturing and representing textures and materials colours (Fig. 5.4) is another crucial aspect of faithfully replicating the look and feel of real-world environments supporting more immersive and authentic experiences to users.

Indeed, the proper representation of textures has the potential to enable realistic simulation of surfaces, such as considering the roughness of plaster walls, the smoothness of tissue, or the grain of marble.

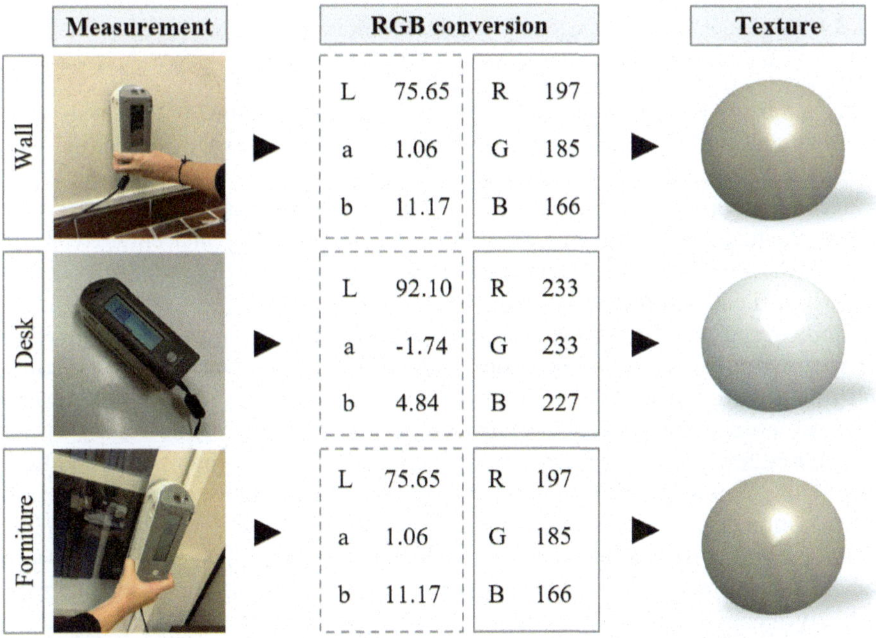

Fig. 5.3 Generation of the texture for the virtual model from real measurements

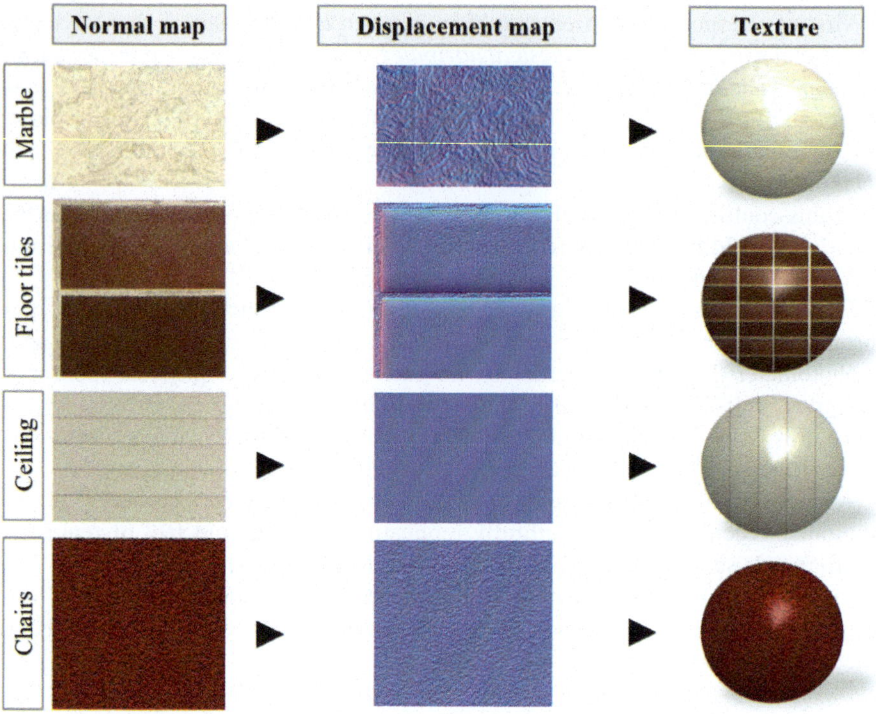

Fig. 5.4 Generation of the texture for the virtual model from real textures

As a result, this meticulous representation allows virtual objects to closely resemble and mimic their real counterparts in detail and nuances, providing users with an enhanced sense of familiarity.

Secondly, appropriate software should be selected to create a 3D model representing the real space with the highest level of detail ensuring an accurate representation of the whole characteristics in terms of room geometry (i.e., walls, floor, door) and layout (i.e., furniture, workstations).

Moreover, *advanced software and hardware* are needed to create a final immersive experience for users, including virtualizing software (e.g., Unreal, Unity engines) and graphics processing units suitable to render high-quality graphics. Textures and materials need to be applied to enhance the model realism while setting up and adjusting lighting source parameters to simulate the real environmental conditions. Eventually, the model can be rendered to produce high-quality visualizations. The virtualization occurs with the implementation of *the first-player control* opting for a virtual camera component suitable to handle head tracking. This feature allows the camera and the model to follow and adapt to the player's movements and the player to freely navigate the scene. As a result, necessary scripts need to be coded, for instance, to visualise also the tests sequentially and automatically, and minimising the interactions with the researcher managing the test.

Once the virtual model is completely set from a geometrical, informatic and virtual point of view, the virtual scenarios need to be created according to the experimental design, the dependent and the independent variables.

Finally, a well-performing *Virtual Reality headset* (or Head-Mounted Display, HMD) must be selected to properly experience the Virtual Environment. A special focus should be given to the resolution image per eye, the pixel density, the illumination expressed in cd/m^2, the refresh rate, the field of view range per eye and the possibility of adjusting the interpupillary distance.

The illustrative example was developed to investigate work efficiency, comfort and behaviour in the Real and Immersive Virtual office Environment. The tasks and questionnaires to be completed by the participants are presented on the virtual computer monitor, respectively, as attached timed videos and sequences of images, to provide the highest level of realism and avoid the break-in-presence in the response collection, while supporting external-ecological validity. The position of the camera was set at 1.10-m height from the ground based on the average eye height of a seated person.

This comprehensive approach is essential to enhance the effectiveness and reliability of the validation process by ensuring that the virtual model accurately replicates its real-world counterpart. Data collected from participants can then be collected and compared between the real-world and the virtual office settings, providing insights into the validity of Virtual Environments.

5.4 Data Collection

Data collection is the core process of experimental activities. To ensure rigorous and reliable validation studies, it is essential to carry out congruent experimental activity applying consistent schedules and procedures in both settings. This involves recruiting participants and exposing them to either the Real or the Virtual Environment, or both (i.e., independent or repeated-measure design, respectively), one or both environments while collecting all the dependent variables.

To contribute to this goal and ensure the highest level of validation for the Virtual Environment, the adoption of the developed step-by-step methodological framework is the core point.

The experimental procedure adopted for the illustrative example (Fig. 5.5) is based on the framework and guidelines proposed in Chap. 3. Participants were recruited for a one-day test to experience the Real (group 1) or the Virtual Environment (group 2). A random assignment ensured the Internal Validity of the research.

At the beginning of each test visit, participants were introduced to the test environment, signed a consent form, received instructions about the experiment and completed the pre-experiment questionnaire. This stage should last at least about 15 min to allow them to get used to the environmental conditions and to reduce any fluctuation related to the 30 min-prior-test physical activity that might have influenced their metabolic rate [2].

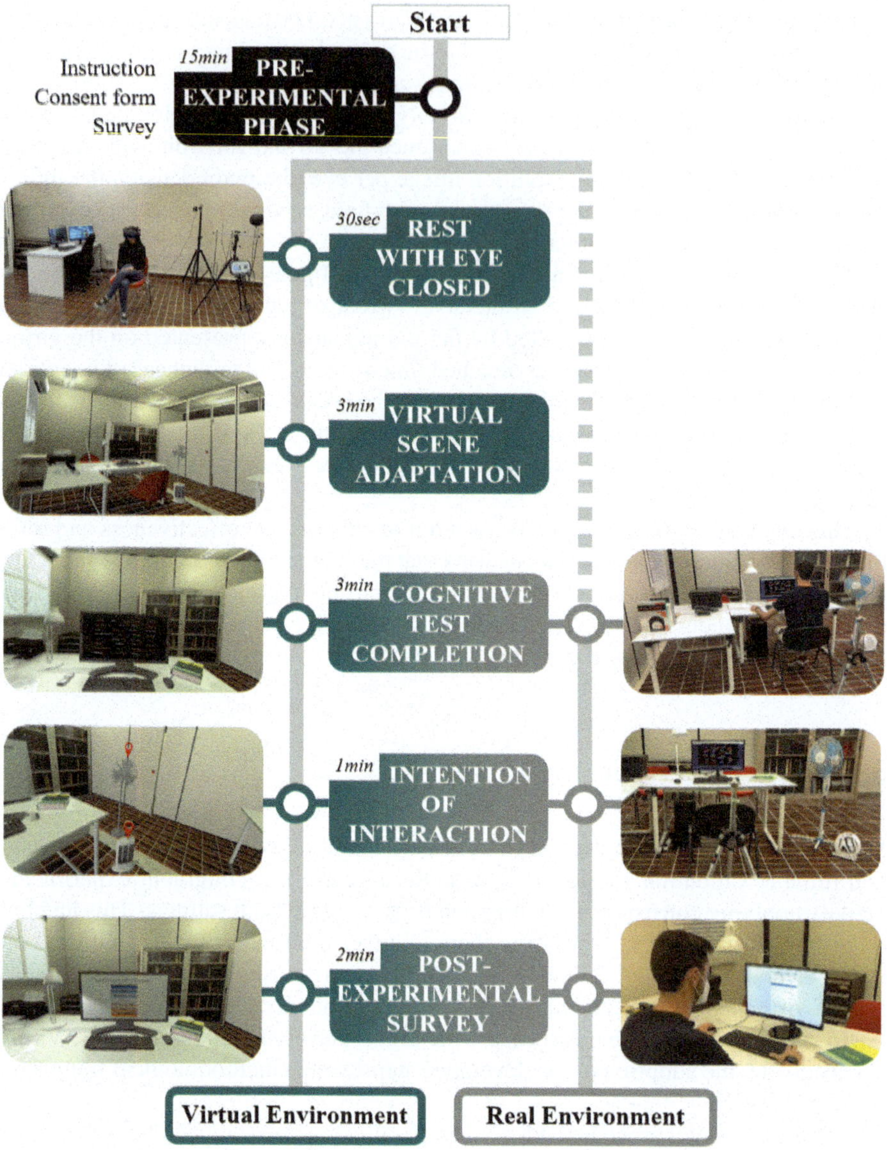

Fig. 5.5 The experimental schedule in the virtual and real environment

The test session in the virtual environment required wearing and setting up the VR head-mounted display and an adaptation phase composed of a rest period with eyes closed and the virtual scene exploration to reduce any psychological fluctuations related to the VR exposure and facilitate immersion, respectively.

In both settings, participants performed the three selected cognitive tasks to investigate the work-efficiency construct. Tasks order randomization (e.g. *M-P, OSPAN, Stroop* vs *Stroop, M-P, OSPAN*) allowed the reduction of the order effect, counterbalancing time-related factors and supporting internal validity. Participants' interaction with the building system (i.e., heater, fan, air conditioner, window) and responses to the post-experimental questionnaire were recorded. In the Virtual and Real Environment tasks and surveys were presented seamlessly on the virtual and real computer monitor, respectively.

This rigorous approach enables the researcher to fulfil all the validity types contributing to the robustness of collected data at the base of further outcomes that can support the validation of the Virtual Reality.

5.5 Benchmarking Real and Virtual Environments

As a final step, the comparison of data collected within the experimental activities between the virtual environment and its real counterpart is essential to confirm the ecological and criterion validity of the findings.

5.5.1 Ecological Validity

Firstly, the researcher needs to check the Ecological Validity of the Virtual Environment to ensure it can adequately represent the real-world setting assessing how well the VE simulates the conditions and responses of the real one.

This includes the analysis of participants' feedback concerning their sense of presence and immersivity and cybersickness symptoms. Specifically, the selected indicators of Graphical Satisfaction (GS), Spatial Presence (SP), Involvement (INV), and Experienced Realism (REAL) are examined and compared with the resulting scores of the literature. Rescaling attributes may be a fundamental step for the effective comparison across studies, transforming the rating to a 5 or a 7-point scale.

Another crucial aspect is the analysis of the cybersickness symptoms which might be caused by the Virtual Environment, the device or the testing activity and the personal susceptibility of participants. In general, researchers should pay attention to high disorder levels. Indeed, insight gathered from participants who experienced cybersickness should be excluded from the overall dataset in order not to negatively affect the reliability of the results. Specifically, reported "vertigo" may indicate a discrepancy between perceived and experienced movement and it is more frequent to be detected if participants are asked to virtually move in the Virtual Environment while standing in the test room. Tests carried out in static conditions are more likely not to cause vertigo. Symptom like "eyestrain" is usually related to "difficulty in focusing" probably suggesting technical issues such as low display resolution and slightly blurred images presented by the head-mounted display. Those are the most common disorders across participants. Hardware issues, uncomfortable head-mounted displays, rapid camera movements or sudden changes in perspective, and prolonged exposure without adequate breaks can trigger symptoms like "general discomfort" "fatigue", and "headache". However, if reported symptom levels are negligible (scores assigned to "not at all" or "slightly"), a positive and comfortable experience for users is highlighted.

Concerning the illustrative example, successful results and effective representation are provided in Figs. 5.6 and 5.7 The average scores for GS (4.58), REAL (4.47), SP (4.21), and INV (4.15) exceed moderate levels equal to 4 on the 5-point Likert scale, indicating high user satisfaction and immersion. In addition, these results surpassed scores from previous studies, confirming an excellent sense of presence and immersivity within the virtual environment.

The cybersickness analysis did not reveal high disorder levels, except for 25% of participants reporting moderate difficulty focusing due to the slightly blurred images presented by the head-mounted display which caused eyestrain (10%). Those

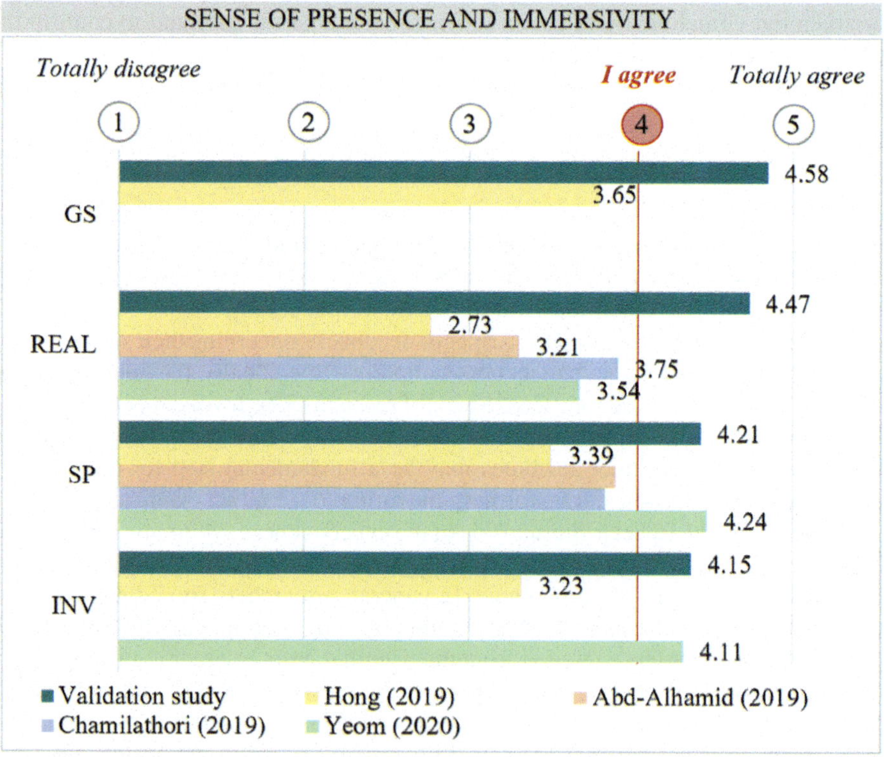

Fig. 5.6 Analysis of the sense of presence and immersivity of the illustrative example (Yeom [3], Chamilothori [4], Abd-Alhamid [5], Hong [6])

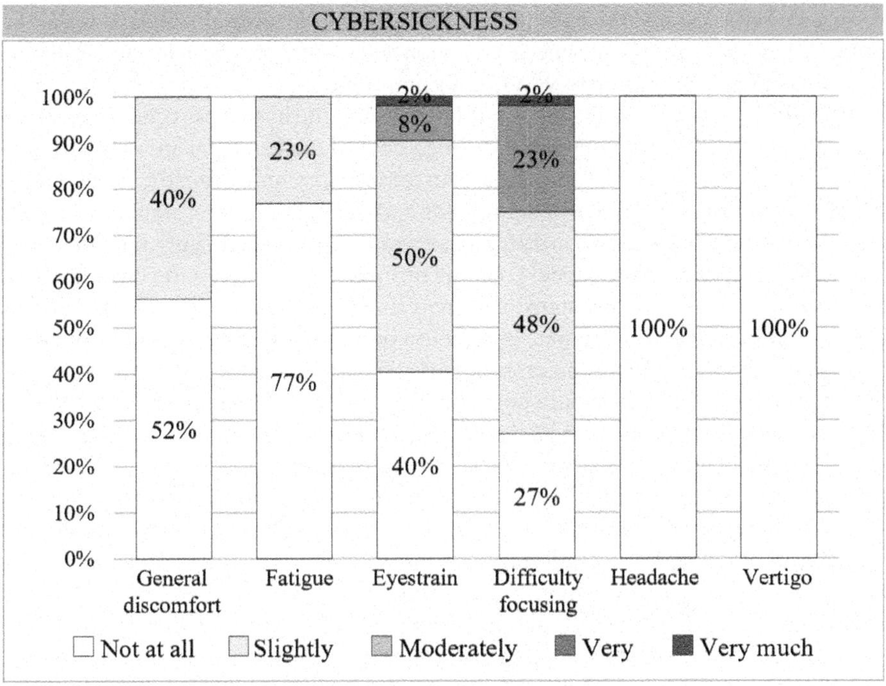

Fig. 5.7 Analysis of the cybersickness ratings of the illustrative example

outcomes allowed the verification of the Ecological Validity of the case study indicating that subjects were properly immersed within the virtual model, which is essential to ensure the reliability of results, particularly in establishing cause-effect relationships.

5.5.2 *Criterion Validity*

Once the Ecological Validity is established, the author proceeded by benchmarking the constructs of interest (e.g., task, comfort, behaviour, perception, physiological parameters) between the virtual and the real-world settings to assess the degree of similarity and consistency between them. Indeed, the aim of Criterion Validity is to evaluate the alignment of obtained results. If no differences in the outcomes are detected and the cause-effect relationships are satisfied, then, the overall validation of the Virtual Environment against its real counterpart is concluded. It is recommended to establish the hypothesis before the experimental design phase depending on the aim of the study to properly gather data collection and analysis effectively.

In a validation study, the hypothesis to be tested to confirm the Criterion Validity deals with looking for the absence of differences in outcomes between experimental conditions (Real Environment vs Virtual Environment).

Initially, to get an overview of possible outcomes the hypotheses can be evaluated qualitatively with *descriptive statistics* (e.g., central tendency, mean, standard deviation). Then, it is of utmost importance to adopt *inferential statistics* to determine whether results are statistically significant and support the interpretation of those hypotheses such as looking for differences among data, quantifying the effect size, developing, and validating models, and quantifying effects given the desired significance level [7]. A primary statistical analysis should assess the normality of the dataset and subsequently compute parametric or non-parametric tests to evaluate the hypotheses. Specifically, in the presence of subjective ratings, non-parametric tests and rank-ordered datasets should be involved due to the ordinal nature of the dataset [8]. Critical values, depending on the significant level, the degree of freedom and p-values are mandatory to determine the statistical significance of the outcomes, if any, between the environmental stimuli of interest, such as real and virtual environments.

Considering the illustrative example of the virtual and real office rooms, task accuracy, thermal and visual comfort responses, intention of interaction and Theory of Planned Behaviour assessment were compared between the two environments to determine the extent to which outcomes collected in the virtual environment differed from the real ones. T-tests were used to compare cognitive task results, while non-parametric tests like the Mann–Whitney U-Test to assess differences in comfort ratings and interaction between real and virtual environments (Tables 5.1 and 5.2). Through a rigorous statistical analysis, a sufficient degree of similarity (p-values above the threshold of 0.05) was detected revealing the absence of influence of the environment type on the participants' cognitive functions, comfort, and behavioural responses.

Additionally, a focus on the predictive ability of the framework presented in this book and Immersive Virtual Environment can be crucial for ultimately confirming

Table 5.1 The results of the unpaired-sample t-test on the cognitive tests

Construct	Dependent variable	t-value	p-value	$\Delta\mu$ RE-IVE
Stroop test	Number of errors in the colour naming	1.70	0.09	−0.23
	Speed of execution	1.74	0.08	−2.31
Magnitude-Parity test	Number of errors in the classification of The digits even/odd and greater/lower than "5"	0.35	0.73	0.06
OSPAN test	Number of errors in the true/false string	0.52	0.60	−0.06
	Number of errors in letters memorised	1.59	0.12	−0.37
	OSPAN score	1.97	0.05	−0.50

Table 5.2 The results of the Mann–Whitney test between RE and IVE on the thermal and visual comfort and number and type of interaction (Z-crit = ±1.96)

Construct	Dependent variable	U-value	Z-value	p-value
Thermal comfort	Thermal sensation vote	1134	−1.80	0.07
	Thermal comfort vote	1578	1.83	0.06
	Thermal preference vote	1179	−1.54	0.12
Visual comfort	Visual sensation vote	1547	1.84	0.06
	Visual comfort vote	1305	−0.46	0.65
	Visual preference vote	1166	−1.83	0.07
Behaviour	Number of intentions of interaction	1456	0.98	0.32
	Type of intentions of interaction	1273	−0.68	0.49

Criterion Validity and the suitability of Virtual Environments for Building Occupant Research. In this context, Confirmatory Factor Analysis, linear regression or linear mixed models can be adopted to analyse for instance the Theory of Planned Behaviour construct within both real and virtual settings. Indeed, by examining specific constructs such as knowledge about energy consumption, awareness of consequences, attitude toward energy-related behaviour, and perceived behavioural control, researchers can gain insights into the factors influencing individuals' behaviour in both RE and IVE.

For instance, results (Table 5.3) of the Confirmatory Factor Analysis and linear regression model applied to the illustrative example indicated an enhancement of predictive power in the prediction model when combining knowledge about energy consumption with awareness and attitude toward behaviour. Knowledge about energy consumption emerged as a significant predictor in both environments of the variation in interaction intention with the absence of significant differences in the predictive ability of the Theory of Planned behaviour between the real and the virtual environments.

Table 5.3 The results of multiple linear regression analysis in the real and virtual office room

Model	Predictors	Predictive power		F-statistics		p-value	
		RE	VE	RE	VE	RE	VE
#1	Consequences (C)	0.02	0.03	0.33	0.35	0.45	0.44
#2	C + Attitude (A)	0.10	0.09	0.87	0.82	0.52	0.57
#3	C + A + Knowledge (K)	0.17	0.17	1.96	1.95	0.04	0.04
#4	C + A + K + Perceived Control (PC)	0.17	0.17	1.96	1.95	0.04	0.04
#5	K	0.12	0.11	3.33	3.34	0.01	0.01

Key observations and results of the illustrative example comparing a real and a virtual office room pinpointed the effectiveness of adopting a comprehensive, strict and flexible framework applied to a reliable Virtual Environment, confirming both its Ecological and Criterion Validity. This comparison helps ensure that individuals' responses observed in the virtual setting are consistent with those in the real world.

Notably, the presented validation process enhances confidence in the reliability and relevance of findings derived from virtual experiments, thereby contributing to improving the reliability of Virtual Reality technology for building occupant research.

As a result, Virtual Reality has demonstrated the potential of supporting multi-domain investigations to enhance indoor environments and well-being from the early design stages and offering avenues for a user-centred design approach in the Architecture, Engineering, and Construction sectors.

References

1. I.D. Bishop, B. Rohrmann, Subjective responses to simulated and real environments : a comparison, Landsc. Urban Plan. 65 (2003) 261–277. https://doi.org/10.1016/S0169-2046(03)00070-7.
2. ASHRAE Standard, ANSI/ASHRAE Standard 55–2004: Thermal Environmental Conditions for Human Occupancy, Am. Soc. Heating, Refrig. Air-Conditioning Eng. Inc. 2004 (2004) 1–34.
3. S. Yeom, H. Kim, T. Hong, M. Lee, Determining the optimal window size of office buildings considering the workers' task performance and the building's energy consumption, Build. Environ. 177 (2020) 106872. https://doi.org/10.1016/j.buildenv.2020.106872.
4. K. Chamilothori, J. Wienold, M. Andersen, Adequacy of Immersive Virtual Reality for the Perception of Daylit Spaces: Comparison of Real and Virtual Environments, LEUKOS - J. Illum. Eng. Soc. North Am. 15 (2019) 203–226. https://doi.org/10.1080/15502724.2017.1404918.
5. F. Abd-Alhamid, M. Kent, C. Bennett, J. Calautit, Y. Wu, Developing an Innovative Method for Visual Perception Evaluation in a Physical-Based Virtual Environment, Build. Environ. 162 (2019) 106278. https://doi.org/10.1016/j.buildenv.2019.106278.
6. T. Hong, M. Lee, S. Yeom, K. Jeong, Occupant responses on satisfaction with window size in physical and virtual built environments, Build. Environ. 166 (2019). https://doi.org/10.1016/j.buildenv.2019.106409.
7. G. Chinazzo, R.K. Andersen, E. Azar, V.M. Barthelmes, C. Becchio, L. Belussi, C. Berger, S. Carlucci, S.P. Corgnati, S. Crosby, L. Danza, L. de Castro, M. Favero, S. Gauthier, R.T. Hellwig, Q. Jin, J. Kim, M. Sarey Khanie, D. Khovalyg, C. Lingua, A. Luna-Navarro, A. Mahdavi, C. Miller, I. Mino-Rodriguez, I. Pigliautile, A.L. Pisello, R.F. Rupp, A.-M. Sadick, F. Salamone, M. Schweiker, M. Syndicus, G. Spigliantini, N.G. Vasquez, D. Vakalis, M. Vellei, S. Wei, Quality criteria for multi-domain studies in the indoor environment: Critical review towards research guidelines and recommendations, Build. Environ. 226 (2022) 109719. https://doi.org/10.1016/j.buildenv.2022.109719.
8. L. Gravetter, Frederick; Wallnau, Statistics for the Behavioural Sciences, 2013.

Chapter 6
Successful Application of the Framework for Building Occupant Research

Abstract Building on the previous methodological foundations, this chapter presents how to successfully employ the developed framework and the validated model to carry out Virtual Reality-based research. This will provide trustworthy evidence about the human dimension in indoor built environments allowing the researcher to make general conclusions and further support building design practices and theories. As the fundamental aim underpinning this book revolves around the potential of adopting Virtual Reality technology to detect the influence of indoor environmental characteristics on humans, special attention is given to the exploration of several stimuli in multi-domain applications. At first, two cross-effect study types with variations of thermal and acoustical stimuli are presented (Sects. 6.1 and 6.2), investigating for completeness the same-modality effect of those conditions. Secondly, Sect. 6.3 presents a combined-effect study type in which the effect of multiple stimuli in combination on individuals' responses (i.e., visual and acoustical dimensions), was assessed focusing on a salutogenic design approach.

6.1 Example 1: Varying the Thermal Environment

To illustrate the applicability of the developed framework and validated model, this section presents a cross-effect case study. The first investigated stimulus involves manipulating the *indoor thermal environment*. Why prioritize thermal variations?

The response lies from decades of field studies assessing the thermal experience of indoor occupants, which have contributed to the development of Fanger's theory [1] and the later adaptive hypothesis [2]. Occupants' response to indoor air temperature changes has been investigated in terms of comfort, behaviour, and physiological responses (e.g., Ref. [3–5]). Such thermal comfort studies showed common traditional research methods (e.g., controlled environmental conditions in labs or climatic chambers, types of collected data) suitable for translation into Virtual Environment experiments. Additionally, cross-modal effects of thermal conditions on visual or acoustic responses have been analysed (e.g., Ref. [6–8]) although with unclear outputs [9].

A. Latini, *Immersive Virtual Reality for a Building Occupant-Centric Design*, Digital Innovations in Architecture, Engineering and Construction,
https://doi.org/10.1007/978-3-031-66028-3_6

Due to the simplicity of modifying the visual dimension in virtual settings, previous VR-based experiments have predominantly investigated the influence of visual domain and indoor layout variations on individuals, with a limited assessment of thermal adaptive behaviour. Nevertheless, recently, the idea to combine controlled indoor environments for thermoception studies and Virtual Environments emerged offering participants new opportunities to experience the so-called mixed-Immersive Virtual Environments (m-IVEs) [10].

Some previous attempts are present in the thermal domain to validate Virtual Reality [10–12] and explore individuals' responses in multi-domain VR-standalone studies by combining different stimuli [13, 14] and cross-modal experiments [14, 15]. Despite that, unresolved issues on experimental protocols have led to inhomogeneous results (e.g., not fully comparable methods) [10] and a lack of behavioural analysis regarding thermal settings [16]. Therefore, the first illustrative example presented in this chapter arises from the need for further research aiming at clarifying the nature of the human-thermal stimuli interaction and providing the effectiveness of the proposed framework and validated model.

Hence, two typical indoor winter discomfort scenarios were set up as the independent variable of this study: a hot (24 °C) and a cold (16 °C) indoor environment. The overall methodological approach to demonstrate the effective applicability of the framework in the presence of thermal variations is presented in Fig. 6.1. Despite the previous successful validation of the model, Ecological Validity needs to be again assessed due to the different participant samples. The results of cognitive tests, thermal and visual comfort ratings, and behaviour were compared between the two thermal conditions and with the findings of previous literature to make general conclusions. In the presence of statistical differences within the dependent variables and cause-effect relationships, the Criterion Validity of the virtual model in addressing the effects of thermal variation is then established.

6.1.1 E1: Experimental Design

52 volunteers (26 male, 26 females, 74% under 30, 94% statistical power with medium effect size and 80% probability) were recruited to perform the cognitive tests (i.e., Stroop test, OSPAN test, Magnitude-Parity test) and answer questionnaires about thermal comfort, visual comfort, sense of presence and immersivity cybersickness disorders and building system intention of interactions to improve thermal comfort. Participants did not experience a dynamic visual change after expressing the intended behaviour and could not perceive the thermal outcome. The experiments followed the prescription established by the experimental framework and adopted the validated virtual model and the schedule of the experiments carried out for validation purposes with no modifications. The indoor thermal environmental conditions were used as a within-subject factor with the same participant exposed to both the thermal variations while keeping constant the surrounding office space. The sample

1 Thermal stimuli and the virtual environment

► **Hot Virtual Environment (H)**	Selection of a winter discomfort scenario with high indoor air temperature (24°C)
► **Cold Virtual Environment (C)**	Selection of a winter discomfort scenario with low indoor air temperature (16°C)

2 Investigation on users' response to varying thermal environment in a mixed-IVE

► **Reported presence and immersivity**	evaluation of perceived presence in the virtual environment
► **Reported cybersickness**	evaluation of perceived sickness after using headset
► **Perceptual accuracy**	evaluation of perception in H and C (thermal comfort, visual comfort)
► **Behavioural accuracy**	evaluation of adaptive behavioural strategies in H and C
► **Task accuracy**	evaluation of accuracy in H and C across three cognitive tests

Fig. 6.1 Illustration of the methodological approach in Example 1

was divided into two balanced groups randomly performing both experimental conditions with a one-week interval between trials, ensuring balanced representation and Internal Validity.

The indoor air temperature, relative humidity and air velocity were recorded throughout the experimental sessions in a position located immediately behind the seated participants performing the test (Fig. 6.2). Concerning indoor air temperature, the average values were 15.84 ± 0.90 °C in the cooler condition and 24.45 ± 0.37 °C in the warmer one.

6.1.2 E1: Summary of Findings

The analysis and the comparison of the four indicators (i.e., Graphical Satisfaction, Experienced Realism, Involvement, Spatial Presence), revealed that the Virtual Environment created an excellent level of presence and immersivity, with most participants experiencing minimal cybersickness disorder levels. This result suggests that users properly felt involved in the Virtual Environment, supporting its Ecological Validity as an effective tool for properly identifying the influence of indoor environmental variations.

Data about cognitive task accuracy, comfort and adaptive behaviour strategies were insight through parametric t-test and non-parametric Wilcoxon signed-rank test, respectively (significance level equal to 0.05) to evaluate if Virtual Reality can

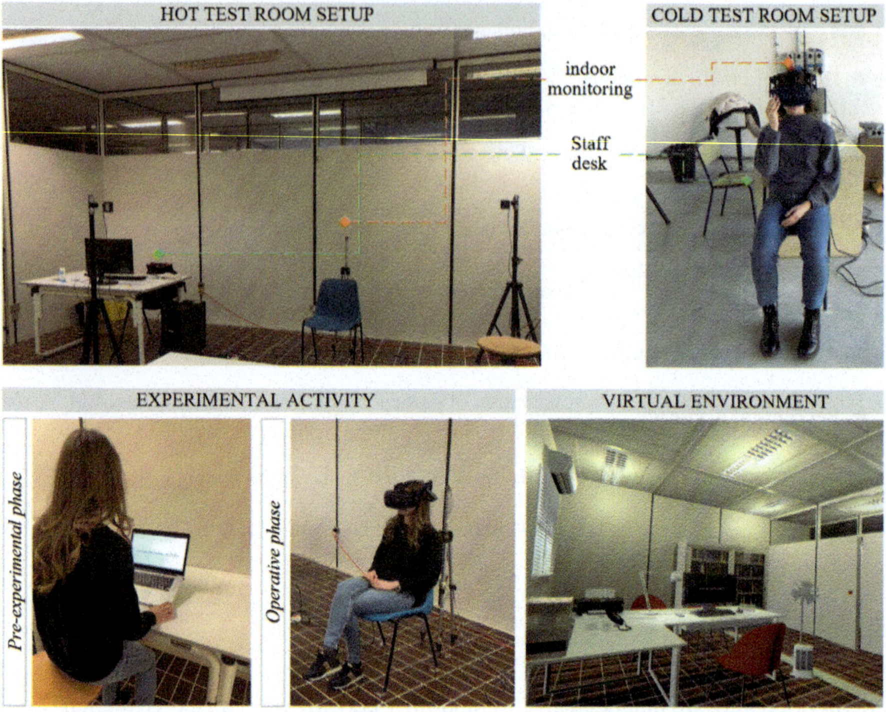

Fig. 6.2 Experimental setup and participants during test session of Example 1

adequately reflect the influence of thermal states deriving from in situ stimuli on individuals' responses. This study evaluated both a same-modality effect (thermal domain—thermal response) and a cross-modal effect (thermal domain and visual response). The independent variable (temperature set-point), while not influencing cognitive functions (task-switching, inhibition, working memory, p-values > 0.05), has a significant impact on thermal comfort and type of adaptive interactions with the building system (p-value < 0.05, Fig. 6.3). In the cooler office condition, 84% of the subjects felt at least «slightly cold» and «cold», while in the warmer condition, 90% felt «slightly warm» and «warm». In particular, participants rated both the thermal conditions to be equally uncomfortable, because the selected indoor air temperature conditions were about ± 4 °C far from the typical winter thermal comfort temperature, around 20 °C.

Significantly different strategies to adapt thermal comfort were detected: at least 77% of participants would have modified the indoor climatic environment by opening the window (65%) and turning on the heater (60%), in warmer and cooler environments, respectively. These have been identified as the best feasible strategies that the subjects would use to improve their thermal sensation in the higher temperature environment, to decrease the indoor temperature and enhance air change, and in the lower temperature environment, respectively (Fig. 6.4).

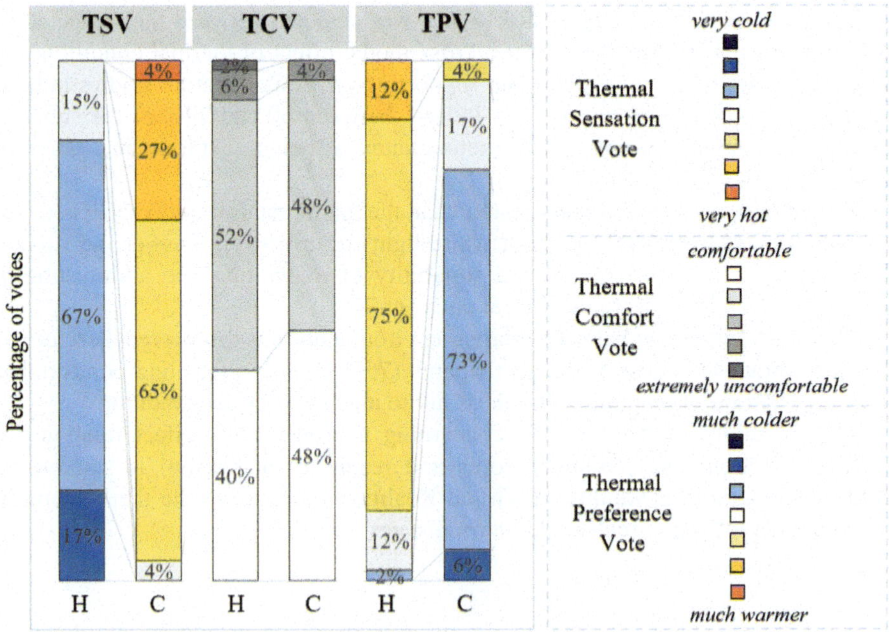

Fig. 6.3 Results of Example 1 concerning thermal comfort votes within the two experimental conditions (16–24 °C)

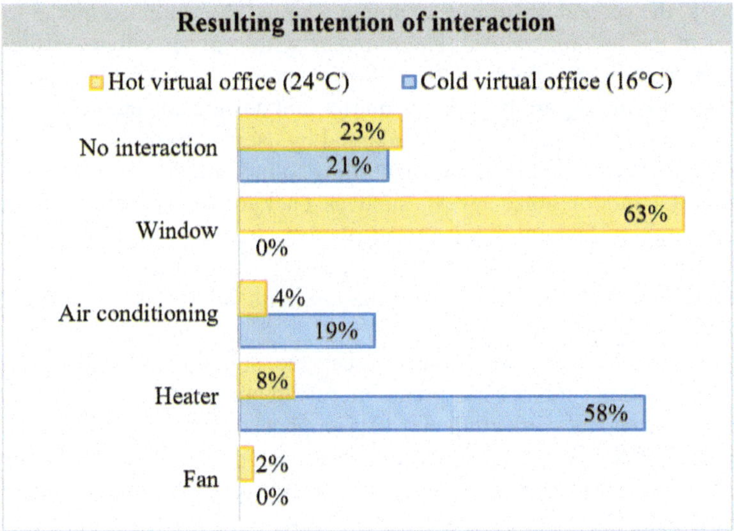

Fig. 6.4 Results of Example 1 concerning intention of interaction within the two experimental conditions (16–24 °C)

The consistency in visual comfort votes was detected between the temperature conditions revealing the absence of a cross-modal effect of thermal conditions on visual response (p-values > 0.05) and supporting previous literature studies in both virtual [12, 14] and real settings [8]. Indeed, between 60 and 79% of the subjects evaluated the light-correlated colour temperature as being «neutral» and «slightly cool».

Interestingly, the researchers noted that the participants rapidly checked the virtual ambient light (4000 K, cool white light) to effectively answer the survey. This supports the effectiveness and suitability of integrating and administrating questionnaires directly into the virtual environment.

The same agreement between thermal environments was discovered also for the comfort parameter, most of the participants (75–81%) report feeling comfortable with 58–69% expressing the willingness not to alter their visual condition.

The reliability of these results concerning a proper cause-effect relationship (thermal environment—comfort scores and resulting interaction) is suitable to confirm the Criterion Validity of Virtual Reality in supporting the thermoception domain and replicating real-world thermal states [11, 17].

6.2 Example 2: Varying the Acoustical Environment

To showcase the flexibility and the successful application of the framework presented in this book, the second illustrative example adopted the validated model to explore variations in the *indoor acoustic environment* within a standalone Virtual Reality crossed-effect study design.

Office environments are becoming smarter and despite advantages in controlling lighting and thermal conditions to be adapted by users and for users, noise remains challenging to control and modulate according to individual preferences.

Detrimental indoor noise levels, such as background speech, ventilation and air conditioning equipment, unanswered phones, and office machinery, have been recognized as a relevant issue since they cause unwanted distractions, stress and dissatisfaction within the office environment with a 66% drop in performance [6, 18–20].

Recent research focused on sound source type, sound pressure level, and reverberation time underscores a widespread interest in studying how the office acoustic environment influences work efficiency [21] emphasizing the need for effective sound masking strategies as a vital priority in office design. This will have the potential to achieve a high degree of occupant comfort and work efficiency. In addition, the cross-relationship between individuals and acoustical factors should be refined to clarify not only the individual influence of each factor alone but also their interaction. However, there's a lack of comprehensive crossed-effect studies design examining the interplay between sound levels and other domains, such as thermal and visual perception [9] which has been limitedly assessed in traditional studies.

In this research context, the use of Virtual Environment has been predominantly devoted to "visually" design a space.

In order to achieve a heightened level of realism and immersivity, it is imperative to improve also the auditory experience of individuals in virtual contexts. Several sets of indoor spaces can be simulated and experienced through audio and video using head-mounted displays [22]. Consequently, there is a growing interest in adopting immersive sound simulations to study the effect of building acoustics on individuals, even though limited studies are currently available often considering on single cognitive function at a time in combined studies of visual and acoustical domains [22–25].

Therefore, research focusing on the evaluation of the cross-modal effect of *Acoustic Virtual Reality* (AVR) on multiple cognitive functions and comfort is lacking, representing a novel area in virtual reality research.

Based on these findings, the experimental study presented in this book chapter (summary in Fig. 6.5) explores the effectiveness of the modelled AVR in terms of sense presence and immersivity and cybersickness ratings (Ecological Validity), as well as investigates the influence of a virtual acoustic environment on users' cognitive performance and thermal comfort within a temperature-controlled Immersive Virtual Environment (Criterion Validity). Specifically, a "quiet environment" without ambient noise serves as the reference for acoustic comparison against a "noisy environment". Five disrupting sound sources were selected as the sound samples of typical office noises to generate a binaural soundtrack integrated into the virtual model. The results of cognitive tests, thermal, visual and acoustical comfort ratings were compared between the two acoustical conditions and with the findings of previous literature to make general conclusions. In the presence of statistical differences in the dependent variables and cause-effect relationships, the Criterion Validity of the virtual model in addressing the effects of acoustical variation is then established.

6.2.1 E2: Experimental Design

A total of 104 participants (52 male, 52 females, 83% under 30, 81% statistical power with medium effect size and 80% probability) were recruited to perform the cognitive tests and answer questionnaires about thermal and acoustical comfort, sense of presence and immersivity cybersickness disorders under a controlled constant indoor air temperature (24.45 $\pm$ 0.48 °C).

Participants visually experienced the validated office model and underwent a single test session randomly assigned to the "quiet" or the "noisy environment" (independent-measure or between-subject design).

The validated office model was integrated with sound stimuli in correspondence to the first player control (Fig. 6.6) derived from field measurements, incorporating five representative sound sources with well-known disrupting effects on cognitive performance: [18, 20–22]: phone rings, machine noise of a laptop and a copier, mechanical systems, human-based sounds and acoustical effects of the closing door.

1 Acoustical stimuli in the virtual environment

► **Noise Virtual Environment** (N)	selection, recording and measurement of five disrupting sound sources (phone rings, machine noise, mechanical systems, human-based sounds)
► **Quite Virtual Environment** (Q)	selection, recording and measurement of non disrupting sound sources (mechanical systems)

2 Identifying the effect of indoor noise through Acoustic Virtual Reality

► **Reported presence and immersivity**	evaluation of perceived presence in the Immersive Virtual Environment
► **Reported cybersickness**	evaluation of perceived sickness after using headset
► **Task accuracy**	evaluation of accuracy in Q and N across three cognitive tests
► **Perceptual accuracy**	evaluation of perception in Q and N (sound distinction, acoustical and thermal comfort)

Fig. 6.5 Illustration of the methodological approach in Example 2

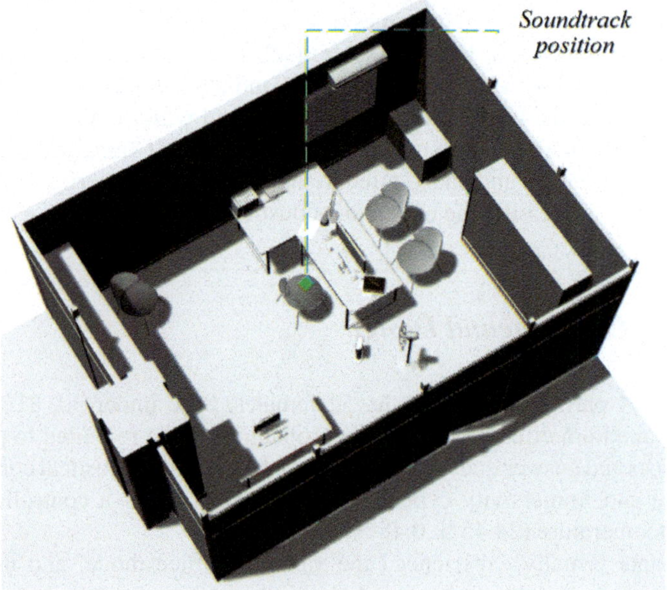

Fig. 6.6 Location of the soundtrack in the office model

Recordings to generate virtual audio stimuli and measurements of the acoustical environment were conducted using a portable recorder and binaural microphone in a real office room resembling the virtual one. The noise samples were mixed into a stereophonic-WAVE format soundtrack with an average L_{Aeq} of 55.6 dB(A) and a sample rate of 44,100 at 16 bit/s. Psychoacoustic characteristics of the sound source were analysed in terms of loudness, sharpness, and fluctuation strength according to ISO 532-1:2017 [26], by using a head and torso simulator and related software. The reverberation time of the room was also calculated according to UNI EN 12,354–6:2006 [27], considering the features of the real office environment adopted for validation purposes, such as its localisation (i.e., suburban area), background noise (external ambient noise level between 40 and 50 dB(A) during daytime), geometry, and materials (no acoustic treatment, plastered walls, tiled floor, flat ceiling, wooden and plastic furniture) to account for the acoustic absorption.

The psychoacoustic parameters of the binaural soundtrack are presented in Fig. 6.7.

Each experimental session lasted approximately 25 min, following the protocol outlined in the developed framework with participants additionally asked to rate their perception of the virtual sound environment according to ISO 12913-2:2018 [28] and ITU-R BS 1116-3:2015 [29] standards.

6.2.2 E2: Summary of Findings

The analysis of Graphical Satisfaction (4.64), Experienced Realism (4.51), Involvement (4.29), and Spatial Presence (4.18) indicators and the presence of minimal cybersickness disorder levels (27% of participants claimed difficulty in focusing) indicated a strong sense of engagement in the virtual environment.

A strong acoustical sensory congruency (Fig. 6.8) was also detected with participants identifying the most distinguishable sound sources as phone rings (96%), machine noise (58%), mechanical systems noise (17%), human-based sound sources (13%), and acoustical effects (4%). This outcome underscores the ecological validity of the Acoustic Virtual Reality model with significant potential in accurately capturing the impact of indoor acoustical environmental variations on individuals (Fig. 6.8).

The parametric t-test and non-parametric Mann–Whitney test were used to extract insight about task accuracy and comfort assessment, respectively, comparing the acoustical conditions to evaluate whether Virtual Reality accurately represents the impact of acoustical conditions elicited by a virtual-world stimulus. This study evaluated both a same-modality effect (acoustical domain—acoustical response) and a cross-modal effect (acoustical domain and thermal response).

The independent variable (acoustical scenario) has a significant disrupting impact on cognitive functions (p-values > 0.05) with a 10% increase in speed of execution for the inhibition task, a 59% decrease in performance observed for task-switching and a 53% decrease for working memory, consistent with previous studies [18–24, 30, 31].

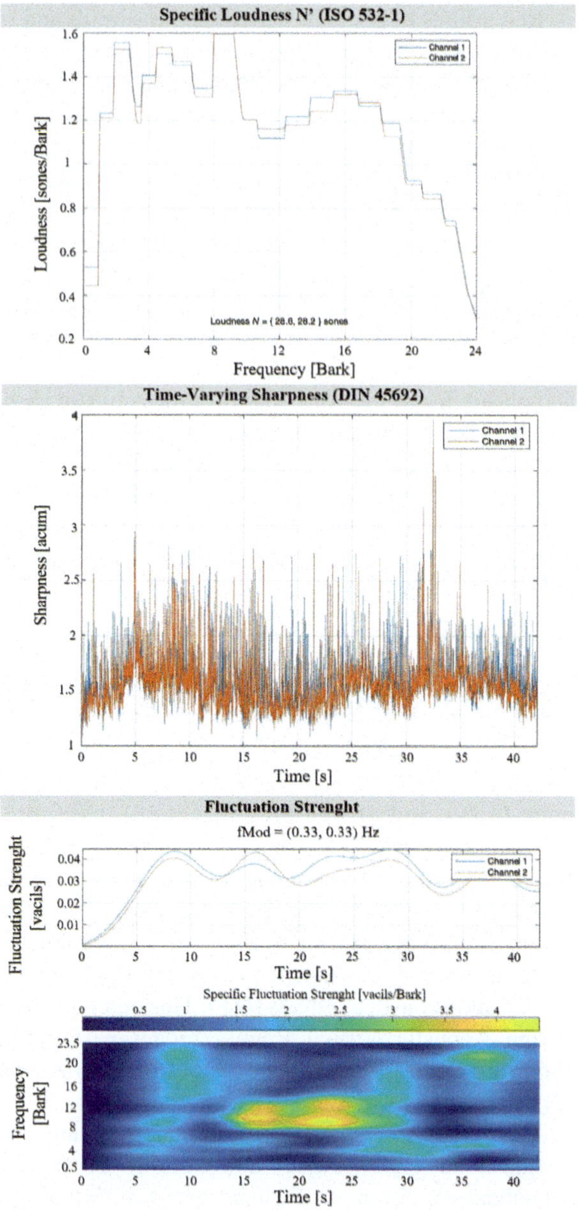

Fig. 6.7 Overview of some of the psychoacoustic parameters of the binaural soundtrack (Channel 1 = right year, Channel 2 = left year)

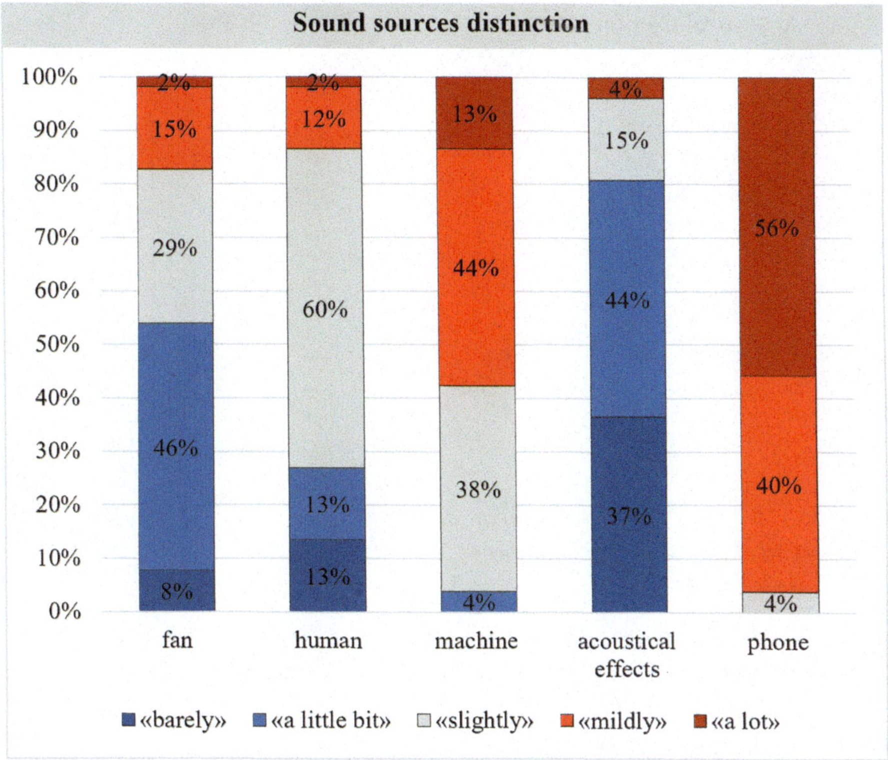

Fig. 6.8 Results of Example 2 concerning the assessment of sound sources distinction

The negative influence of acoustics on task accuracy was supported by participants' self-reports (Fig. 6.9). Indeed, 98% of participants evaluated the virtual sound environment as being chaotic (96%), boring (27%), not «pleasant», «relaxing» or «calm» and «uncomfortable» as a result. Moreover, the overall sample expressed that the acoustical environment could influence productivity highlighting a strong correspondence between the results of the tests, the self-reports and the awareness of the effect of the acoustical environment on work efficiency.

The independent variable while not influencing thermal sensation and preference votes (p-values > 0.05, Fig. 6.9) has a significant impact on thermal comfort ratings. Participants rated the thermal condition as 44% more uncomfortable under «noisy conditions», likely due to the psychological impact of the disruptive noise.

Since the tool reflects the theoretical expectation and cause-effect relationship about the effect of acoustics on work efficiency and thermal and acoustical comfort scores, the Criterion Validity of Acoustic Virtual Reality in supporting investigation and simulations in the acoustical domain is then confirmed.

The reliability of these findings highlighted the potential of the proposed Acoustic Virtual Reality to further deliver effective user-centred design analysis and strategies

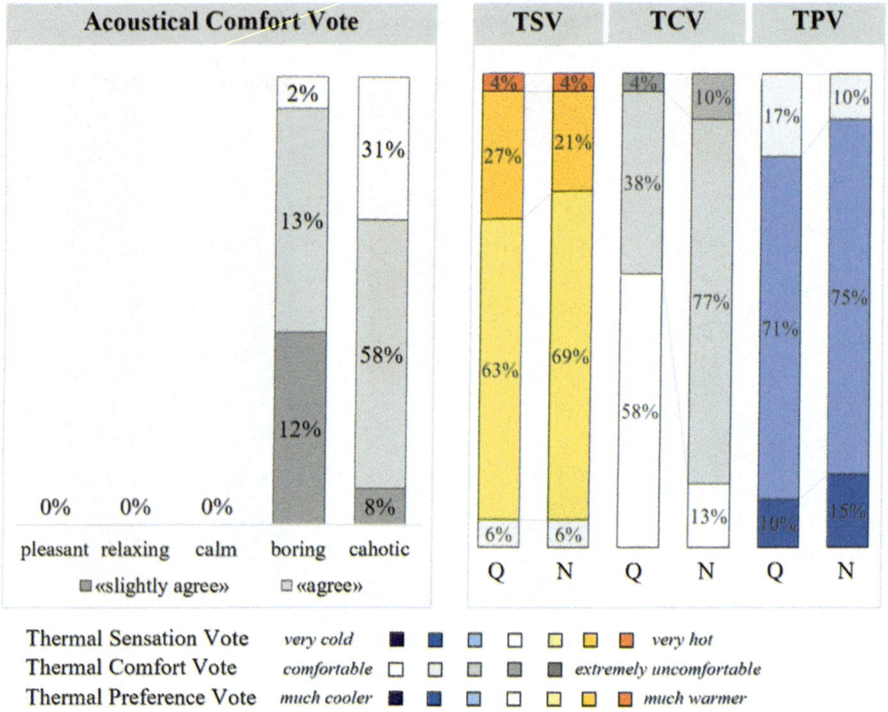

Fig. 6.9 Results of Example 2 concerning acoustical and thermal comfort votes

additionally in the acoustical domain. This provides users with multi-sensory Virtual Environments with audio-visual rendering integrated within the technology itself which enhances the users' immersion.

6.3 Example 3: Combining Visual and Acoustical Variation

The final case study concerns the integration of visual and acoustical variation within the validated virtual office environment presenting a shift in perspective toward a salutogenic and users-centred design approach [32]. Namely, the trigger for the stimuli choices depended on the concept that human-dimension depends not only on the absence of environmental problems or diseases but also on the presence of attributes that can promote positive effects on well-being, task performance, and physiological and perceptual responses.

In this context, numerous studies have demonstrated that exposure to *natural elements* is associated with positive outcomes, in particular: enhanced health and well-being with anxiety and stress reduction, positive physiological responses (e.g., decrease in skin temperature conductance, deceleration of heart rate in response to a more relaxed status), increased positive emotions and cognition [33, 34]. That is why, the World Green Building Council framework [35] for healthy and green offices and Green Building Rating Standards increasingly supported *Biophilic Design* intervention in a sensorial design approach [36]. Indeed, nature's potential can be triggered by several nature-related sensory stimuli (e.g., visual, acoustical, olfactory).

Traditionally, the main attention has been directed towards the *visual connection with nature* (e.g., nature elements in space, natural view from windows) since vision is the primary sense that building occupants use to recognize and process environments and has a relevant influence on the perception of other senses [37]. Additionally, a growing body of literature has highlighted the potential of natural sound sources, like bird songs or flowing water, on individuals' responses to provide useful masking, improved privacy and positive affective outcomes [38]. However, recent studies showed how both sound and visual interaction affect perception and demonstrated that auditory perception improves when accompanied by visual cues, and vice versa sounds can improve attention to related visual elements [39, 40]. Thus, a holistic approach to study the multisensory nature of human perception in indoor built environments should be adopted with increasing attention to understanding the combined visual and acoustical components and their interactions.

Biophilic Design studies based on Virtual Reality tools representing indoor environments are still limited, mainly focused on single-domain studies on stress and anxiety levels reduction [41–44], self-emotion assessment [45–47], thermal state [41], single [45] or multiple cognitive tests [48, 49]. Hence, underdeveloped is the application of Immersive Virtual Environments to support researchers in understanding the potential effects of visual and non-visual (acoustical) connection with nature on human work efficiency and comfort through a multi-domain approach. Therefore, the third illustrative example presented in this chapter arises from the need for further multi-domain research aiming at a comprehensive evaluation of work efficiency potentials, changes in physiological responses and influence on attention and concentration in task execution adopting eye-tracking technology. Hence, nine combined audio-visual virtual scenarios were set up (overall methods in Fig. 6.10) to focus on the multi-sensory interaction of Biophilic Design interventions in office environments demonstrating the suitability of the new methodological approach based on Virtual Reality.

6.3.1 E3: Experimental Design

A 3 × 3 factorial design was employed with three between-participants levels of Visual Factor office layout (i.e., Indoor Green, Outdoor Green, Non-Biophilic) and three within-participants levels of Acoustic Factor (i.e., Office, Office + Traffic, Office + Nature sounds). The experimental design followed the recommendations and guidelines of the developed framework. Test sessions counterbalanced the presentation order of acoustic stimulus, with subjects randomly assigned to a visual scenario (66 participants per Visual Factor level).

Visual Factor	Selection and creation of three virtual visual scenarios: Non-Biophilic, Indoor Green, Outdoor Green
Acoustical Factor	Selection, recording and measurement of three acoustical scenarios: Office, Office + Traffic, Office + Nature
1	Effectiveness of VR to investigate Biophilic Design research interventions
▶ **Reported presence and immersivity**	evaluation of perceived presence in the virtual environment
▶ **Reported cybersickness**	evaluation of perceived sickness after using headset
2	Effect of audio-visual connection with nature on cognitive performance
▶ **Task accuracy**	evaluation of accuracy in the three cognitive tests across combination of Visual Factor * Acoustic Factor
3	Effect of audio-visual connection with nature on soundscape assessment
▶ **Perceptual accuracy**	evaluation of perceived affective quality of soundscape in office environments across combination of Visual Factor * Acoustic Factor
4	Effect of audio-visual connection with nature on physiological response
▶ **Physiological response**	evaluation of physiological responses across combination of Visual Factor * Acoustic Factor
5	Effect of audio-visual connection with nature on visual attention and distraction
▶ **Visual attention**	evaluation of the visual attention (eye-tracking metrics) to greenery across the levels of Visual Factor during the adaptation phase
▶ **Visual distraction**	evaluation of the visual distraction (eye-tracking metrics) induced by the presence of greenery during the task execution
▶ **Task accuracy**	evaluation of the relationship between eye-tracking responses and the task accuracy across the levels of Visual Factor during the task execution evaluation of accuracy in the three cognitive tests across the levels of Visual Factor

Fig. 6.10 Illustration of the methodological approach in Example 3

Concerning the development of the soundtracks (Fig. 6.11), the sound material was recorded with a First Order Ambisonics tetrahedral microphone and measured at 1.2 m in a real office environment of similar floor plan, door and window sizes to the simulated one ($T30_{500\text{–}2\,\mathrm{k\,Hz}} = 0{,}30$ s). The office condition was recorded in the presence of four people performing office-type activities. The traffic and natural

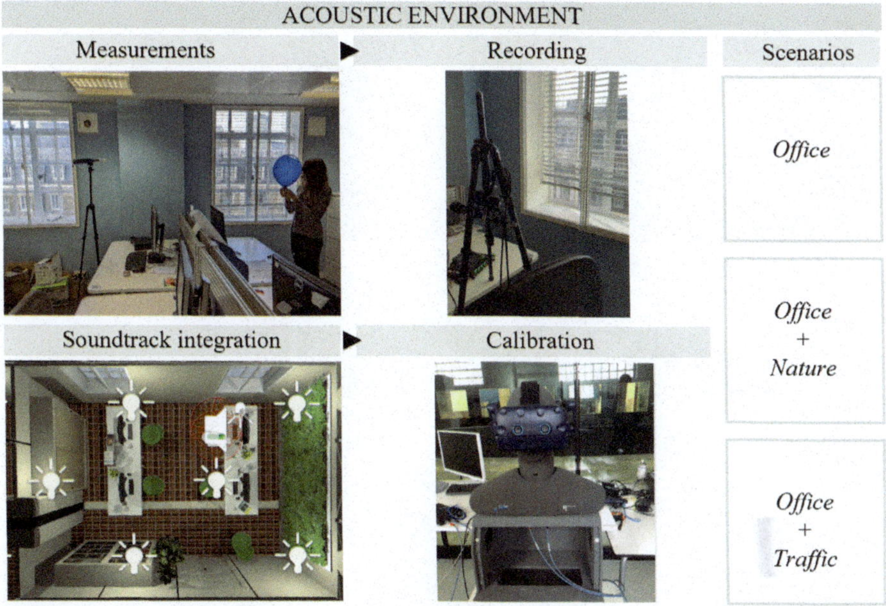

Fig. 6.11 Generation of the acoustic environment and related scenarios to be integrated into the Immersive Virtual Environment

sound conditions, consisting mainly of birdsong, were recorded in the same environment, unoccupied, and with windows open to outside traffic. All the recordings were edited to obtain 1-min excerpts and then transformed to an AmbiX B-format and presented via headphones integrated into a head-mounted display.

The playback level was set through the binaural head and torso simulator with the exact headphones and the Virtual Reality head-mounted display used in the experiment, with the simulation running and at the listener in the centre of the simulated sound field ($L_O = 45$ dB(A), $L_{O+T} = L_{O+N} = 54$ dB(A)).

The validated model (Chap. 5) constituted the basic Non-Biophilic (NB) scenario. Two additional scenarios were created based on Biophilic Patterns principles [50] and the WELL Building Standard recommendation [51], incorporating elements such as a living wall (covering a wall area equal to 60% of the floor area) and potted plants (covering 4% of the floor area) for Indoor Green and a natural view of trees for Outdoor Green. Figure 6.12 presents the Immersive Virtual Environments scenarios. The sitting position within the virtual model ensured the subjects a View Factor of outdoor equal to 5.

The Unity Oculus Spatializer package provided an immersive soundscape experience through the head-tracking binaural rendering of the acoustic environment. The soundtracks were implemented within the VR model in correspondence with the first player control which was also the position where measurements and recordings took place in the real office room. In addition, to gauge participants' visual attention, the Virtual Environment was integrated with iMotion software.

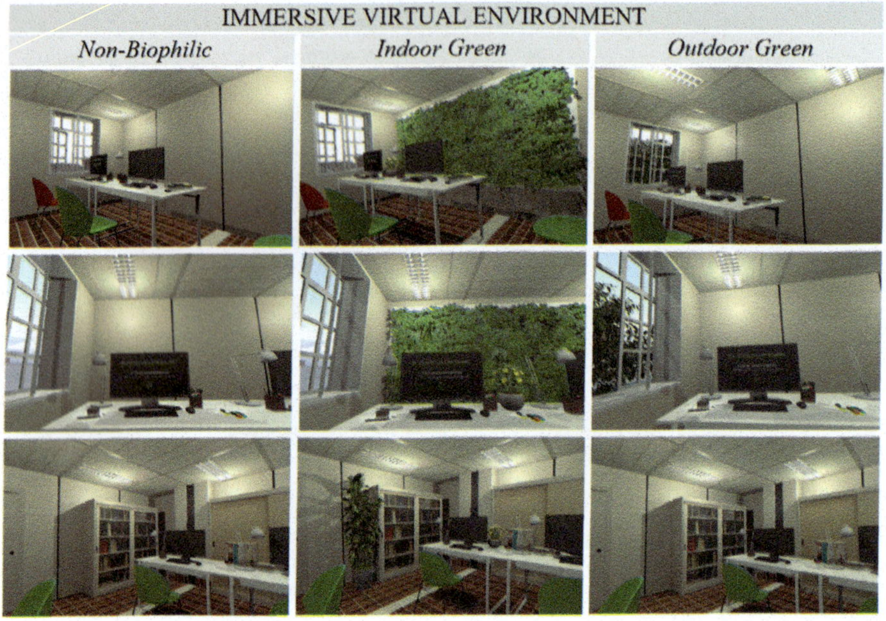

Fig. 6.12 Visual scenarios in the Immersive Virtual Environment and generation of the acoustic environment and related scenarios

Throughout the experiment, indoor environmental conditions (i.e., air and operative temperature, humidity, air velocity) and physiological signals through wristbands (i.e., Electro-Dermal Activity, Pulse Rate, Skin Temperature, Eye-tracking metrics) were monitored.

The experimental procedure (Fig. 6.13) followed the indication of the validated framework and involved 198 participants in a one-day test of 35 min each performing cognitive tests, soundscape and virtual model assessments for each acoustical scenario in random order with 30 s of rest with eyes closed among them.

6.3.2 *E3: Summary of Findings*

A consistent and logical spatial representation of the office room from a visual point of view and the sensory congruency about the direction and distance of sounds from an acoustic term was detected. Indeed, during the adaptation phase, participants verbally described the features of each experienced acoustical scenario, as follows:

- in the Office (O) condition, the majority of participants identified typical workplace noises associated with «keyboard», «laptop», «mouse», «typing» (70%), and «telephone noise» (13%) as coming from the inner side of the virtual room.

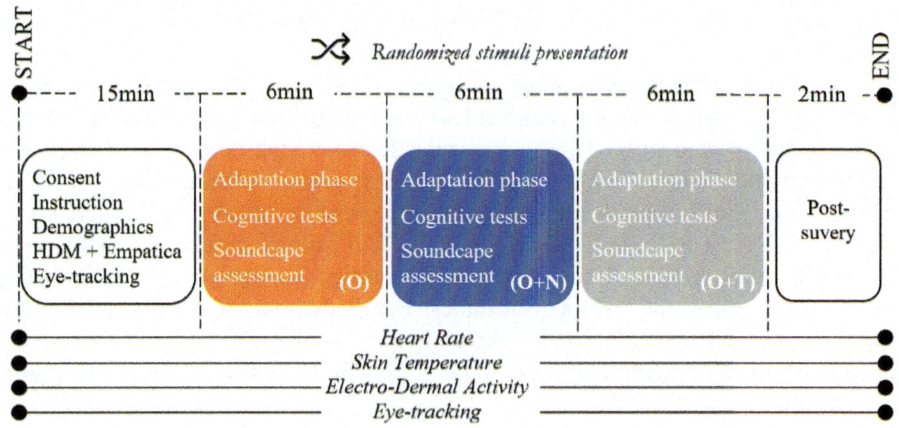

Fig. 6.13 Experimental procedure of Example 3

Human-based sounds like unintelligible «speech» (31%) and «steps» (6%) were also detected.

- Concerning the Office + Nature (O + N): 100% of participants identified the "natural sounds" of "birds" coming from the open «window» on the left-hand side of the office. Indoor office sounds were also identified by 61% of participants.
- In the Office + Traffic (O + T) scenario, "traffic", "road", "cars", "buses", and "horn" noises were identified by the whole sample as coming from the open "window" on the left-hand side of the office. Indoor office sounds were also identified by 50% of participants, slightly lower than in the O + N conditions since traffic sounds seemed more predominant.

The outcomes of the sense of presence and immersivity and cybersickness disorders confirmed the Ecological Validity suggesting the effectiveness of Virtual Reality as an effective tool for preliminary evaluation of the potential of biophilic interventions and then the reliability of participants' responses.

Data about cognitive task accuracy, perceptual responses and physiological signals were insight through Generalized Linear Mixed-Effects Models considering the visual layout and acoustic scenarios as fixed effects and participants as random factors.

Results highlighted that visual and acoustical connections with nature can positively contribute to shaping a more supportive office environment through the adoption of Virtual Reality tools and effective experimental framework. Indeed, *greater accuracy in the three cognitive tests* occurred when participants were exposed to both visual and acoustical natural elements, while they performed worse in the presence of traffic noise. In particular, the Acoustic Factor exhibited a higher improvement effect compared to the visual one, between 23 and 71% against 12–39%. Moreover, in a user-centred design approach, the best visual*acoustic condition for improving participants' work efficiency occurred in the Indoor Green condition combined with Natural sounds.

Concerning the *perceptual dimensions* (Fig. 6.14), a primary significative effect of the acoustic domain on the pleasantness and eventfulness attributes [28, 52–54] was detected (p-value < 0.05). The reference acoustic condition (Office noise) was rated by participants as being uneventful (76%), slightly pleasant and somewhat monotonous. Traffic sounds coming from open windows can cause an increase in eventfulness and a decrease in pleasantness (81%), resulting in a chaotic soundscape. Conversely, the addition of natural sounds in an office environment can improve the overall pleasantness (86%) and eventfulness (i.e., increased vibrancy) (58%) of the space. Interestingly, pleasantness toward natural sounds increased in the presence of indoor greenery, while Outdoor Green is beneficial in moderating traffic noise perception.

Results from *physiological signals* revealed also significant insights into the effects of visual and acoustic stimuli on sympathetic nervous system activation linked to stress and anxiety levels [55–57]: a more relaxed status is indicated by high Skin Temperature and low Electro-Dermal Activity and Pulse Rate values as

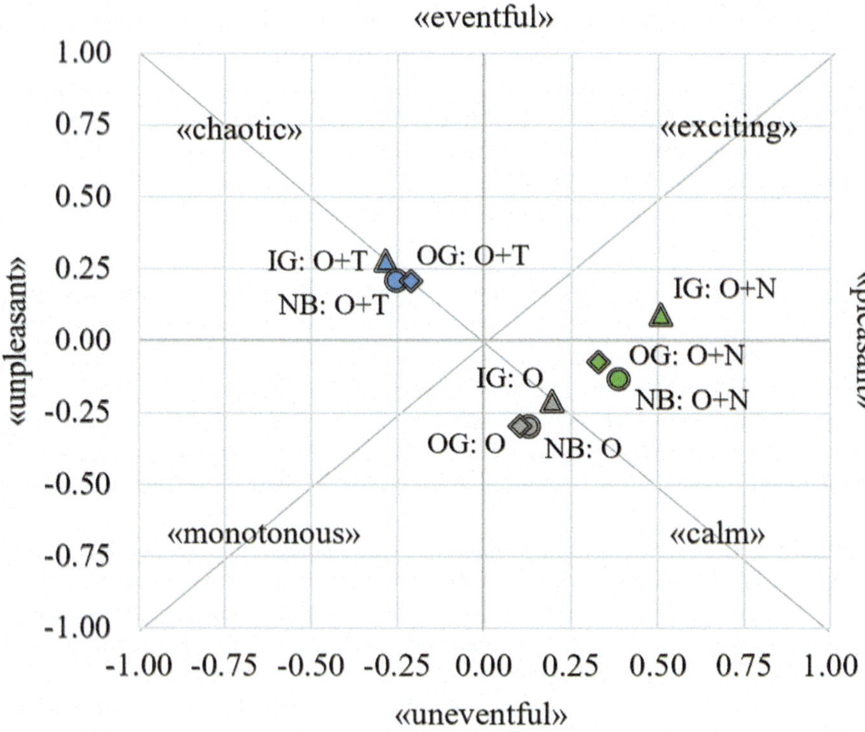

Fig. 6.14 Median values of soundscape assessment for each tested scenario [NB—Non-Biophilic, IG—Indoor Green, OG—Outdoor Green, O—Office, O + T—Office + Traffic, O + N—Office + Nature]

the parasympathetic nerve is activated. In general, the Acoustic Factor (η^2 between 0.91 and 0.94) had a higher magnitude effect compared to that of the Visual Factor ($\eta^2 = 0.78$). Considering Electro-Dermal Activity and Pulse Rate, exposure to pleasant soundscapes in the presence of acoustical connection with nature has the potential to decrease more the recorded signals compared to unpleasant ones (traffic condition) which trigger stress, increasing sympathetic nerve activity ($p < 0.05$). In the presence of a visual connection with nature, a significant reduction in Electro-Dermal Activity was highlighted in Indoor Green settings compared to Outdoor Green and Non-Biophilic scenarios (p-value < 0.05). Conversely, a limited effect was detected on Pulse Rate and no relevant results concerned Skin Temperature, which can be potentially induced by a short 6-min exposure to each acoustical condition.

Particularly noteworthy were the *eye-tracking* findings indicating that exposure to visually natural elements resulted in a lower level of cognitive load and a more efficient search for the correct information enhancing task accuracy (e.g., much less time to read and complete the task, fewer errors).

The analysis of fixation counts, duration (Fig. 6.15) and eye-movement scan paths revealed that the proximity of users to the natural element induced the highest visual attention during the pre-experimental phase (i.e., the nearer the object the higher the visual attention). Conversely, the visual distraction from tasks was influenced by the spatial location and dimension of the greenery (i.e., the larger the object the more it potentially distracts the users).

This result is in contrast with the cognitive performance results revealing a higher accuracy in the presence of greenery elements. Thus, the presence of green elements during the task execution does not disrupt individuals' cognitive performance while increasing the overall interest in the indoor environment. Since participants briefly shifted their attention to the green elements, the result can be interpreted as the subjects' need for a mental break to allow attention restoration from the cognitive load associated with the tests. In the presence of tasks requiring a high cognitive load, greenery acts as an "irrelevant distractor". Indeed, the cognitive effort necessary to visually process green elements may be minimal in comparison with the huge amount of cognitive load required to complete the task. As a result, the cognitive performance of participants was not disrupted. This completely aligns with the Attention Restoration Theory and the potential of the nature view to capture attention, allowing the brain regions to be restored and potentially preventing fatigue during task completions serving as short breaks.

Dealing with the major complexity of this book, the successful application of the protocol has been demonstrated in fully Immersive standalone Virtual Environments. The fundamental challenge in adopting Immersive Virtual Reality to support Building Occupants Research was addressed by demonstrating the possibility of enhancing the overall realistic perception of users by integrating and combining the visual dimension provided by Virtual Reality with the thermal and acoustical one.

The experiment results of the three case studies demonstrated that the proposed framework enables the development of an effective and efficient testing procedure to apply Virtual Reality in further analysis and deliver valid and generalisable results.

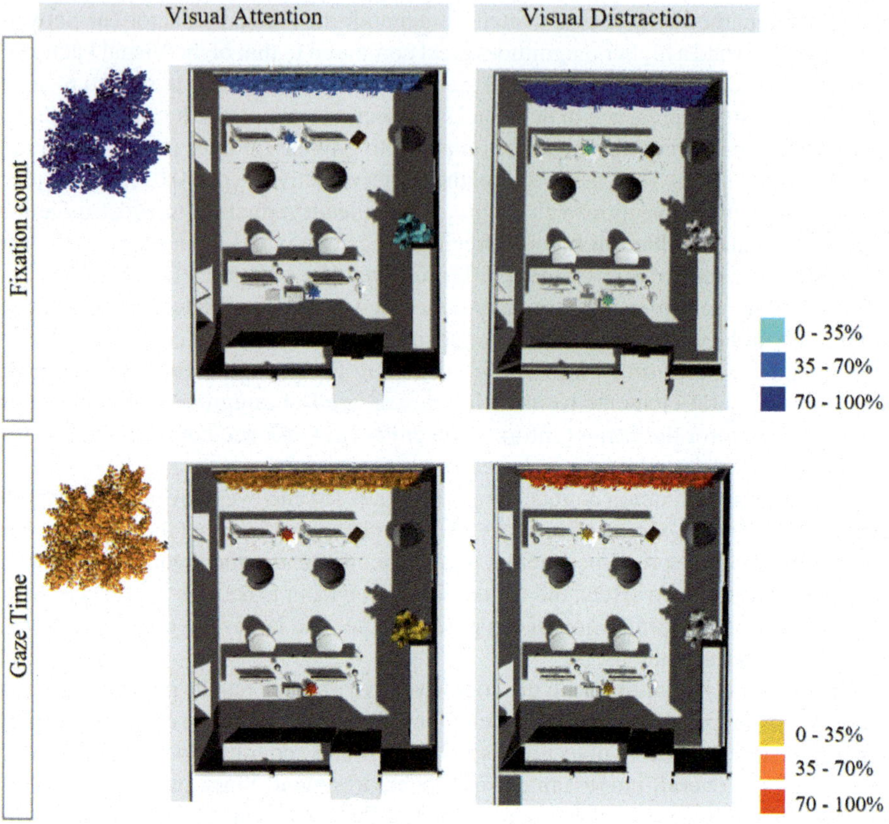

Fig. 6.15 Participants' attention and distraction in percentage terms of fixation counts and duration

By effectively and fully integrating the users in computer-generated scenarios, properly developed Immersive Virtual Environments have the potential to replicate the effect of multiple independent variables (also combined) on the dependent variables (cognitive, perceptual and behavioural, psychological, and physiological response).

This kind of finding expands the range of usability of the framework and the validated model with the potential of strengthening and facilitating research about human-building interaction through multi-sensory analyses carried out in standalone Virtual Environments coupled with other stimuli.

This is a fundamental step to highlight the potential of Virtual Reality as a cost-effective and flexible tool for investigating the human-dimension, enabling Building Occupant Research applications particularly related to multi-domain studies that may not be feasible in laboratory-based studies or physical settings and supporting decision-making strategies for indoor design.

References

1. P.O. Fanger, Thermal Comfort: Analysis and Applications in Environmental Engineering, New York, 1970.
2. R.J. de Dear, G.S. Brager, Developing an Adaptive Model of Thermal Comfort and Preference Richard, ASHRAE Trans. 104 (1998) 145–167.
3. L. Huang, Y. Zhu, Q. Ouyang, B. Cao, A study on the effects of thermal, luminous, and acoustic environments on indoor environmental comfort in offices, Build. Environ. 49 (2012) 304–309. https://doi.org/10.1016/j.buildenv.2011.07.022.
4. G. Chinazzo, R.K. Andersen, E. Azar, V.M. Barthelmes, C. Becchio, L. Belussi, C. Berger, S. Carlucci, S.P. Corgnati, S. Crosby, L. Danza, L. de Castro, M. Favero, S. Gauthier, R.T. Hellwig, Q. Jin, J. Kim, M. Sarey Khanie, D. Khovalyg, C. Lingua, A. Luna-Navarro, A. Mahdavi, C. Miller, I. Mino-Rodriguez, I. Pigliautile, A.L. Pisello, R.F. Rupp, A.-M. Sadick, F. Salamone, M. Schweiker, M. Syndicus, G. Spigliantini, N.G. Vasquez, D. Vakalis, M. Vellei, S. Wei, Quality criteria for multi-domain studies in the indoor environment: Critical review towards research guidelines and recommendations, Build. Environ. 226 (2022) 109719. https://doi.org/10.1016/j.buildenv.2022.109719.
5. C. Huizenga, S. Abbaszadeh, L. Zagreus, E. Arens, Air quality and thermal comfort in office buildings: Results of a large indoor environmental quality survey, Heal. Build. Creat. a Heal. Indoor Environ. People, Proc. 3 (2006) 393–397.
6. W. Yang, H.J. Moon, Cross-modal effects of noise and thermal conditions on indoor environmental perception and speech recognition, Appl. Acoust. 141 (2018) 1–8. https://doi.org/10.1016/j.apacoust.2018.06.019.
7. C.K.C. Lam, H. Yang, X. Yang, J. Liu, C. Ou, S. Cui, X. Kong, J. Hang, Cross-modal effects of thermal and visual conditions on outdoor thermal and visual comfort perception, Build. Environ. 186 (2020) 107297. https://doi.org/10.1016/j.buildenv.2020.107297.
8. G. Chinazzo, J. Wienold, M. Andersen, Influence of indoor temperature and daylight illuminance on visual perception, Light. Res. Technol. 52 (2020) 350–370. https://doi.org/10.1177/1477153519859609.
9. . Wu, Y. Wu, X. Sun, J. Liu, Combined effects of acoustic, thermal, and illumination on human perception and performance: A review, Build. Environ. 169 (2020) 106593. https://doi.org/10.1016/j.buildenv.2019.106593.
10. S. Saeidi, G. Rentala, T. Rizzuto, T. Hong, N. Johannsen, Y. Zhu, Exploring thermal state in mixed immersive virtual environments, J. Build. Eng. 44 (2021) 102918. https://doi.org/10.1016/j.jobe.2021.102918.
11. G. Ozcelik, B. Becerik-Gerber, Benchmarking thermoception in virtual environments to physical environments for understanding human-building interactions, Adv. Eng. Informatics. 36 (2018) 254–263. https://doi.org/10.1016/j.aei.2018.04.008.
12. A. Latini, E. Di Giuseppe, M. D'Orazio, C. Di Perna, Exploring the use of immersive virtual reality to assess occupants' productivity and comfort in workplaces: an experimental study on the role of walls colour, Energy Build. 253 (2021) 111508. https://doi.org/10.1016/j.enbuild.2021.111508.
13. A. Heydarian, B. Becerik-Gerber, Use of immersive virtual environments for occupant behaviour monitoring and data collection, J. Build. Perform. Simul. 10 (2017) 484–498. https://doi.org/10.1080/19401493.2016.1267801.
14. G. Chinazzo, K. Chamilothori, J. Wienold, M. Andersen, Temperature–Color Interaction: Subjective Indoor Environmental Perception and Physiological Responses in Virtual Reality, Hum. Factors. 63 (2021) 474–502. https://doi.org/10.1177/0018720819892383.
15. A. Latini, E. Di Giuseppe, M.D. Orazio, Development and application of an experimental framework for the use of virtual reality to assess building users ' productivity, J. Build. Eng. 70 (2023) 106280. https://doi.org/10.1016/j.jobe.2023.106280.
16. G. Ozcelik, B. Becerik-Gerber, R. Chugh, Understanding human-building interactions under multimodal discomfort, Build. Environ. 151 (2019) 280–290. https://doi.org/10.1016/j.buildenv.2018.12.046.

17. D. Yeom, J.H. Choi, Y. Zhu, Investigation of physiological differences between immersive virtual environment and indoor environment in a building, Indoor Built Environ. 28 (2019) 46–62. https://doi.org/10.1177/1420326X17731945.
18. Y. Al Horr, M. Arif, A. Kaushik, A. Mazroei, M. Katafygiotou, E. Elsarrag, Occupant productivity and office indoor environment quality: A review of the literature, Build. Environ. 105 (2016) 369–389. https://doi.org/10.1016/j.buildenv.2016.06.001.
19. World Green building Council, Health, wellbeing & Productivity in Offices, World Green Build. Counc. 1 (2014) 46.
20. S.P. Banbury, D.C. Berry, Office noise and employee concentration : Identifying causes of disruption and potential improvements, Ergonomics. 48 (2005) 25–37. https://doi.org/10.1080/00140130412331311390.
21. Q. Meng, Y. An, D. Yang, Effects of acoustic environment on design work performance based on multitask visual cognitive performance in office space, Build. Environ. 205 (2021) 108296. https://doi.org/10.1016/j.buildenv.2021.108296.
22. I. Muhammad, M. Vorländer, S.J. Schlittmeier, Audio-video virtual reality environments in building acoustics: An exemplary study reproducing performance results and subjective ratings of a laboratory listening experiment, J. Acoust. Soc. Am. 146 (2019) EL310–EL316. https://doi.org/10.1121/1.5126598.
23. R. Doggett, E.J. Sander, J. Birt, M. Ottley, O. Baumann, Using Virtual Reality to Evaluate the Impact of Room Acoustics on Cognitive Performance and Well-Being, Front. Virtual Real. 2 (2021) 1–9. https://doi.org/10.3389/frvir.2021.620503.
24. J.Y. Jeon, H.I. Jo, B.B. Santika, H. Lee, Crossed effects of audio-visual environment on indoor soundscape perception for pleasant open-plan office environments, Build. Environ. 207 (2022) 108512. https://doi.org/10.1016/j.buildenv.2021.108512.
25. E.J. Sander, C. Marques, J. Birt, M. Stead, O. Baumann, Open-plan office noise is stressful: multimodal stress detection in a simulated work environment, J. Manag. Organ. 27 (2021) 1021–1037. https://doi.org/10.1017/jmo.2021.17.
26. ISO - International Organization for Standardization, ISO 532–1:2017 Acoustics — Methods for calculating loudness — Part 1: Zwicker method, (2017).
27. ISO - International Organization for Standardization, UNI EN 12354–6:2006 Building Acoustics - Estimation of acoustic performance of buildings from the performance of elements - Part 6: Sound absorption in enclosed spaces, (2006).
28. ISO - International Organization for Standardization, ISO 12913–1:2014 Acoustics — Soundscape — Part 1: Definition and conceptual framework, (2014).
29. ITU-R BS.1116–3, Methods for the subjective assessment of small impairments in audio systems BS Series Broadcasting service (sound), Int. Telecommun. Union. 3 (2015).
30. A. Kaarlela-Tuomaala, R. Helenius, E. Keskinen, V. Hongisto, Effects of acoustic environment on work in private office rooms and open-plan offices - Longitudinal study during relocation, Ergonomics. 52 (2009) 1423–1444. https://doi.org/10.1080/00140130903154579.
31. H. Jahncke, V. Hongisto, P. Virjonen, Cognitive performance during irrelevant speech: Effects of speech intelligibility and office-task characteristics, Appl. Acoust. 74 (2013) 307–316. https://doi.org/10.1016/j.apacoust.2012.08.007.
32. V. Ruohomäki, M. Lahtinen, K. Reijula, Salutogenic and user-centred approach for workplace design, Intell. Build. Int. 7 (2015) 184–197. https://doi.org/10.1080/17508975.2015.1007911.
33. W. Zhong, T. Schröder, J. Bekkering, Biophilic design in architecture and its contributions to health, well-being, and sustainability: A critical review, Front. Archit. Res. 11 (2022) 114–141. https://doi.org/10.1016/j.foar.2021.07.006.
34. S. Kaplan, The Restorative Environment: Nature and Human Experience, in: D. Relf (Ed.), Role Hortic. Hum. Well Being Soc. Dev., Timber Press, 1992: pp. 134–142.
35. WorldGBC, Health & Wellbeing Framework: Six Principles for a Healthy, Sustainable Built Environment. Executive report, (2020) 18. https://worldgbc.org/sites/default/files/WorldGBC Health %26 Wellbeing Framework_Exec Report_FINAL.pdf.
36. B. Jiang, Y. Song, H.X. Li, S.S.Y. Lau, Q. Lei, Incorporating biophilic criteria into green building rating tools: Case study of Green Mark and LEED, Environ. Impact Assess. Rev. 82 (2020). https://doi.org/10.1016/j.eiar.2020.106380.

37. W.H. Ko, S. Schiavon, H. Zhang, L.T. Graham, G. Brager, I. Mauss, Y.W. Lin, The impact of a view from a window on thermal comfort, emotion, and cognitive performance, Build. Environ. 175 (2020) 106779. https://doi.org/10.1016/j.buildenv.2020.106779.
38. S. Felipe Contin de Oliveira, F. Aletta, J. Kang, Self-rated health implications of noise for open-plan office workers: An overview of the literature, Build. Acoust. (2023). https://doi.org/10.1177/1351010X231152841.
39. G.M. Echevarria Sanchez, T. Van Renterghem, K. Sun, B. De Coensel, D. Botteldooren, Using Virtual Reality for assessing the role of noise in the audio-visual design of an urban public space, Landsc. Urban Plan. 167 (2017) 98–107. https://doi.org/10.1016/j.landurbplan.2017.05.018.
40. S. Michaeal, The Sonic Environment of Cities, Environ. Behav. 1 (1969) 49–70. https://doi.org/10.1177/001391656900100104.
41. A. Sedghikhanshir, Y. Zhu, Y. Chen, B. Harmon, Exploring the Impact of Green Walls on Occupant Thermal State in Immersive Virtual Environment, Sustain. 14 (2022). https://doi.org/10.3390/su14031840.
42. S. Yeom, H. Kim, T. Hong, Psychological and physiological effects of a green wall on occupants: A cross-over study in virtual reality, Build. Environ. 204 (2021) 108134. https://doi.org/10.1016/j.buildenv.2021.108134.
43. J. Yin, N. Arfaei, P. MacNaughton, P.J. Catalano, J.G. Allen, J.D. Spengler, Effects of biophilic interventions in office on stress reaction and cognitive function: A randomized crossover study in virtual reality, Indoor Air. 29 (2019) 1028–1039. https://doi.org/10.1111/ina.12593.
44. J. Yin, J. Yuan, N. Arfaei, P.J. Catalano, J.G. Allen, J.D. Spengler, Effects of biophilic indoor environment on stress and anxiety recovery: A between-subjects experiment in virtual reality, Environ. Int. 136 (2020) 105427. https://doi.org/10.1016/j.envint.2019.105427.
45. A. Emamjomeh, Y. Zhu, M. Beck, The potential of applying immersive virtual environment to biophilic building design: A pilot study, J. Build. Eng. 32 (2020) 101481. https://doi.org/10.1016/j.jobe.2020.101481.
46. S. Yeom, H. Kim, T. Hong, H.S. Park, D.E. Lee, An integrated psychological score for occupants based on their perception and emotional response according to the windows' outdoor view size, Build. Environ. 180 (2020). https://doi.org/10.1016/j.buildenv.2020.107019.
47. D. Haryndia, T. Ayu, Effects of Biophilic Virtual Reality Interior Design on positive emotion of university students responses, 2020.
48. J. Yin, S. Zhu, P. MacNaughton, J.G. Allen, J.D. Spengler, Physiological and cognitive performance of exposure to biophilic indoor environment, Build. Environ. 132 (2018) 255–262. https://doi.org/10.1016/j.buildenv.2018.01.006.
49. Q. Lei, C. Yuan, S.S.Y. Lau, A quantitative study for indoor workplace biophilic design to improve health and productivity performance, J. Clean. Prod. 324 (2021) 129168. https://doi.org/10.1016/j.jclepro.2021.129168.
50. W.D. Browning, C.O. Ryan, J.O. Clancy, 14 Patterns ofBiophilic Design: Improving health & wellbeing in the built environment, Terrapin Bright Green. 1 (2014) 1–64.
51. International WELL Building Instituite, WELL v2, 2020. https://v2.wellcertified.com/en/wellv2/overview.
52. Ö. Axelsson, M.E. Nilsson, B. Berglund, A principal components model of soundscape perception, J. Acoust. Soc. Am. 128 (2010) 2836–2846. https://doi.org/10.1121/1.3493436.
53. J.A. Russell, A circumplex model of affect, J. Pers. Soc. Psychol. 39 (1980) 1161–1178. https://doi.org/10.1037/h0077714.
54. B. Posner, Jonathan; Russell, James; Peterson, The circumplex model of affect: An integrative approach to affective neuroscience, cognitive development, and psychopathology, Dev. Psychopathol. 17 (2005) 715–734. https://doi.org/10.10170/S0954579405050340.
55. S. Solhjoo, M.C. Haigney, E. McBee, J.J.G. van Merrienboer, L. Schuwirth, A.R. Artino, A. Battista, T.A. Ratcliffe, H.D. Lee, S.J. Durning, Heart Rate and Heart Rate Variability Correlate with Clinical Reasoning Performance and Self-Reported Measures of Cognitive Load, Sci. Rep. 9 (2019) 1–9. https://doi.org/10.1038/s41598-019-50280-3.

56. B. John T., Cacioppo;Louis G., Tassinary;Gary G., Hanbook of Psychophysiology, Cambridge University Press, 2007.
57. M. Awada, B. Becerik-Gerber, R. Liu, M. Seyedrezaei, Z. Lu, M. Xenakis, G. Lucas, S.C. Roll, S. Narayanan, Ten questions concerning the impact of environmental stress on office workers, Build. Environ. 229 (2023) 109964. https://doi.org/10.1016/j.buildenv.2022.109964.

Chapter 7
Conclusion and Perspectives

Abstract Improving multi-sensory building occupant research and guaranteeing a user-centric approach in building design for more sustainable and supportive buildings for individuals could be reached through an innovative approach based on Virtual Reality. The implementation of an effective, valid, and replicable experimental framework to organise, carry out and enhance the adoption of Virtual Reality technology in research studies could significantly solve these issues. Significant examples of validation and successful applications are provided in this book. However, the potential of Virtual Reality solutions should be extended, and further works are needed. This conclusive chapter summarizes the main achievements and impact on academia, building design, standards and society. Finally, some interesting future steps for researchers in adopting the proposed methodology on a scientific level are presented.

7.1 Innovative Solutions for Building Occupant-Centric Design

The built environment is a pivotal determinant of occupants' health and well-being, influencing their overall quality of life.

With people spending a huge amount of daily time indoors, the need for a supportive, conducive, comfortable and healthy indoor environment has never been more urgent, particularly considering the resulting economic implications of indoor environmental quality. Integrating human factors into building decision-making phases and design is essential for delivering more user-centred and efficient buildings.

In Building Occupant Research, empirical assessments, including in-situ monitoring campaigns and laboratory-based studies, are crucial to gather evidence-based design guidelines.

A significant barrier to the acceleration of knowledge in understanding how multiple indoor environmental conditions influence occupants is the difficulty of controlling the variation of indoor environmental conditions. Indeed, despite recent technological advancements, gaps persist in a scarcity of multi-domain assessments of indoor environments to consider multiple and multisensorial indoor environmental

A. Latini, *Immersive Virtual Reality for a Building Occupant-Centric Design*, Digital Innovations in Architecture, Engineering and Construction,
https://doi.org/10.1007/978-3-031-66028-3_7

characteristics simultaneously. This is due to adopted heterogeneous methodological approaches and cost and time challenges related to the complexity of data collection methods in physical settings and real monitoring campaigns. This causes difficulty in conducting a comprehensive analysis in the human-building context and the impossibility of replicating a wide range of contexts, carrying out analysis for buildings still under design, and customising experimental models by modifying the multiple variables in a short time.

Consequently, the drawbacks are inconsistent and tenuous outcomes with unique site-specific studies, evaluations of human responses could not be free from Ecological Validity issues resulting in limited generalizability to support evidence-based design guidelines, building performance models and theories.

A possible solution could be the implementation of more technological innovations into empirical assessment methods, developing suitable knowledge to support evidence-based design guidelines and a user-centred approach.

Virtual Reality and Immersive Virtual Environments are suggested as an alternative method and effective solutions that can facilitate the exploration of multi-domain assessments and leverage the adoption of advanced tools and experimental approaches to address and improve users' dimensions in building design. These low-cost technologies thanks to the speed execution allow replication of tests and users to be immersed in a 1:1 scaled environment, while researchers collect real-time feedback and easily control the design variables.

Currently, main research gaps and challenges exist in Virtual Reality-based studies which currently harm its adoption to support evidence-based design practices and improve indoor environments for individuals.

These issues are related to single-domain assessments with a scarcity of multi-domain studies, limited attention to validation process and presence, immersion and disorders levels, experiments mainly centred on visual domain and indoor layout variations, few investigations on thermal settings adaptive behaviour, inhomogeneous administration of surveys and comprehensive work efficiency investigations.

In this context, despite a growing interest in Virtual Reality to support Building Occupants' Research, the development of a mature and holistic science of Human-Centric indoor environments is still impeded by the lack of an agreed-upon conceptual framework. Based on these drawbacks, an innovative methodological approach is needed to ensure the validity and generalizability of the research findings while adopting Virtual Reality technology as a "data collector".

In order to give an operative answer to these issues, this book traces the basis of a novel *experimental framework* to organise, carry out and enhance a more aware adoption of *Virtual Reality in Building Occupants Centric Design and research studies*. From this point of view the integration of *Virtual Reality tools, multi-domain approaches, validation types of research design and human-dimension metrics*, will foster user-centred approaches and empower the overall human-building interaction thanks to pre-occupancy assessments.

7.2 Building Occupant-Centric Design and Virtual Reality Approach: Impacts and New Perspectives

The choice of developing *a strict, comprehensive but flexible experimental framework* is a key element of adopting innovative solutions like Virtual Reality and Immersive Virtual Environments to support Building Occupant Research and design effective and supportive indoor environments with time and money saving (needed for real-world activities).

In this context, validated virtual models are reliable and effective ways to perform analysis in different scenarios without the necessity of in-situ tests. A similar requirement is essential while dealing with the complexity of multi-sensory environmental stimuli acting simultaneously on individuals.

On a *scientific level*, this solution can be a step-by-step approach to organise the overall experimental procedures aimed at supplying one of the most important helps for *researchers* to establish a strict experimental design suitable to produce trustworthy data, effectively look for a cause-effect relationship between variables and draw valid general conclusions.

Moreover, as shown by Chaps. 5 and 6, practical suggestions for researchers are very useful in setting up suitable *experimental activities* to ensure data properly representing individuals' responses to their complex surroundings with respect to different environmental stimuli.

Effectiveness and *replicability* are the key features and potentialities of the defined framework.

The primary outcome of having such a methodological valuable instrument is a mitigation of the shortcomings in Virtual Reality-based studies.

Another key aspect is the opportunity to expand the use of Virtual Environments to support the research in the built environment and design practises. By offering a systematic approach to organise, carry out, and validate Virtual Reality experiments, this framework lays the foundation for advancing the science and theories of Human-Centric indoor environments, thus paving the way for future innovations in this field.

From a *building design perspective*, in order to provide an effective aid to designers and professionals, Virtual Reality has to provide *quantitative guidelines for the design phase* offering information for evaluating the influence and level of effectiveness of the decision-making phase.

Indeed, data from Virtual Reality and framework-based solutions are essential in the future convergence of the *Architecture, Engineering and Construction sectors* and advanced technologies and approaches.

Collected evidence can reinforce the role of Virtual Reality to adequately quantify the impacts of design choices on the human dimension support *evidence-based indoor design practices* and could lead to a convergence between prototypes and design simulation.

Professionals are then provided with the basis necessary to couple advanced evidence-based design and building practices.

The resulting design guidelines would be suitable to *encourage not arbitrary design choices* in a variety of built environment practices and to provide *long-term value and quality of life in indoor environments.*

The inclusion of such Virtual Reality-evidence-based knowledge in building systems, design and maintenance is a crucial point to deliver personalised building systems capable of supporting the optimal operation of the building, reducing energy consumption and increasing the overall building system efficiency.

In this context, such evidence-based indoor design practices currently do not include outcomes established by immersive virtual experiments. Thus, at *a building standards level*, this can lead to the development of *new regulations* incorporating Virtual Reality sessions and then supporting a new generation of smart buildings.

On a *social level*, the integration of a valuable experimental framework for Virtual Reality applications in Buildings Occupants Research can provide scientific evidence for the negative and positive impacts of multiple indoor environmental conditions on individuals.

Moreover, this can challenge many current design practices and user-centred services based on oversimplified empirical approaches determining which attributes of the indoor environment matter most to building occupants.

From this point of view, this contribution could allow a more tangible possibility of ensuring a sustainable, acceptable and conducive indoor environment for the health and well-being of the people, providing long-term value and quality of life and facilitating the shift toward a more sustainable paradigm coupled with technological innovation.

However, Virtual Reality and the framework can also be extended to many other issues that involve human responses as fundamental elements of indoor quality levels, energy-saving practices and awareness of behavioural consequences.

For such applications is essential to enrich Virtual Environments with real-time data from Building Management Systems and results from Building Energy Models to support building occupants in the operation of building equipment and adjustment procedures through proper and real feedback.

In the meanwhile, the analysis of behavioural patterns in such applications has the potential to deepen the development of adaptive behavioural models suitable for filling the gaps between real and simulated energy performance.

Virtual Reality simulations also offer a cost-effective way to inform design choices based on specific building needs and user-centric approaches. Integration of Virtual Reality with software systems used in the Architectural, Engineering and Construction sectors, like Building Information Modelling, promises enhanced user-friendly design processes, support decision-making and lifecycle management.

SPRINGER NATURE

GPSR Compliance

The European Union's (EU) General Product Safety Regulation (GPSR) is a set of rules that requires consumer products to be safe and our obligations to ensure this.

If you have any concerns about our products, you can contact us on ProductSafety@springernature.com

In case Publisher is established outside the EU, the EU authorized representative is:

Springer Nature Customer Service Center GmbH
Europaplatz 3
69115 Heidelberg, Germany

The manufacturer's authorised representative in the EU is Springer Nature Customer Service Centre GmbH, Europaplatz 3, 69115 Heidelberg, Germany. If you have any concerns regarding our products, please contact ProductSafety@springernature.com

Printed and bound by CPI Group (UK) Ltd, Croydon, CR0 4YY
30/09/2026
02225469-0001